An Evangelical Response to *Baptism, Eucharist and Ministry*

Edited by Paul Schotenboer

Prepared by the Study Unit on Ecumenical Issues
of the World Evangelical Fellowship Theological Commission

Published on behalf of the
World Evangelical Fellowship by
The Paternoster Press
Carlisle

Copyright © 1992, The Paternoster Press

All Rights Reserved. No part of this publication may
be reproduced, stored in a retrieval system, or
transmitted, in any form or by any means, electronic,
mechanical, photocopying, recording or otherwise,
without the prior permission of the publisher
or a licence permitting restricted copying.
In the U.K. such licences are issued by the
Copyright Licensing Agency, 90, Tottenham Court Road,
London W1P 9HE.

British Library Cataloguing in Publication Data

Baptism, Eucharist and Ministry.
  1. Christian doctrine
  I. Schrotenboer, Paul II. World Evangelical Fellowship
230

ISBN 0–85364–513–2

Typeset by Photoprint, Torquay, Devon,
and Printed in Great Britain for The Paternoster Press,
P.O. Box 300, Carlisle, CA3 0QS
by The Guernsey Press Co. Ltd., Guernsey, Channel Islands.

In 1982 the Commission on Faith and Order of the World Council of Churches met in Lima, Peru, and produced an historic document called *Baptism, Eucharist and Ministry*. This document, commonly referred to as BEM, has elicited perhaps more responses from churches and ecclesiastical organizations than any other document in recent centuries.

The World Evangelical Fellowship has responded to the invitation of Faith and Order to submit an evaluation of the Document, Faith and Order Paper 111. The text of the Evangelical Response is found in this publication.

The Response has been made by the Study Unit on Ecumenical Issues of WEF's Theological Commission. The Study Unit prepared its response over a period of three years. In order to involve evangelical theologians from the various continents, an initial draft was distributed for comment. The comments received testified to the keen interest which BEM has among Evangelicals. When the Study Unit had done its work the document was submitted to the Theological Commission which approved it for submission to Faith and Order.

The WEF Theological Commission is pleased that its contribution will be added to the six volumes of responses which have been printed and that its views will be considered by Faith and Order when it on its part prepares a response to all the responses it has received during the last seven years.

This Evangelical Response has a dual address. It is intended first for Faith and Order. Although there are many Evangelicals belonging to the churches which have officially responded, this response may be considered the position of international Evangelicalism. In making its response, the World Evangelical Fellowship submits its contribution as one of the recognized Christian World Communions.

The second address is to Evangelicals themselves, some of whom have not become deeply involved in ecumenical issues and may stand somewhat to the side of the ecumenical movement. The Study Unit cherishes the hope that the distribution of this Evangelical Response will not only acquaint Evangelicals with this event but also encourage the member fellowships to engage in conversation with others on this significant development. This evaluation represents an endeavour to be active in the movement to advance toward unity in truth.

In submitting this Evangelical Response we have entered into dialogue, one in which there is clear testimony of shared convictions concerning the truth of the Gospel. It is also one that displays a willingness to acknowledge that, along with the firm agreement among Evangelicals on the essentials of the faith, there is a wide variety of viewpoint on the two sacraments and the ministry of the Church. The Response also acknowledges that the Lima Document challenges them to reflect further on their own positions concerning baptism, the Lord's supper and the ministry of the church.

The dialogue affords the benefit of seeing ourselves as others see us. More importantly, it gives us an opportunity of making an obedient response to the Apostle when he said that with all the saints we should seek to grasp how wide and long and high and deep is the love of Christ and to know the love that surpasses knowledge. We need this if we are to be filled to the measure of the fullness of God (Eph. 3:18, 19).

Baptism, Eucharist and Ministry is a part of a larger study by Faith and Order called *Toward a Common Expression of the Apostolic Faith*. The Evangelical Response contained in this publication calls for a companion piece by Evangelicals concerning that continuing study.

We would like to express our deep gratitude to the Commission on Faith and Order of the World Council of Churches for their ready permission for us to include in this booklet the original text of the Lima Document, *Baptism, Eucharist and Ministry*.

Paul G. Schrotenboer
Study Unit Convener

Members of the WEF *Ecumenical Issues Study Unit:*

Dr Henri Blocher (France)
Revd Pietro Bolognesi (Italy)
Dr Donald A. Carson (USA)
Rvdo Jose M. Martinez (Spain)
Dr David Parker (Australia)
Dr Charles A. Tipp (Canada)
Dr George Vandervelde (Canada)
Dr Miroslav Volf (Yugoslavia)
Dr Paul G. Schrotenboer (USA)

An Evangelical Response to *Baptism, Eucharist and Ministry*

Edited by Paul Schrotenboer

Prepared by the World Evangelical Fellowship, June 1989.

Preamble

Faith and Order Paper No. 111, the Lima document on *Baptism, Eucharist and Ministry* (BEM), has been widely acclaimed as a most significant statement in the recent history of the church. It represents a momentous endeavour to reach doctrinal agreement on key issues that for centuries have troubled the churches. The World Evangelical Fellowship welcomes the opportunity to join those many churches and organizations that are responding to the document and sharing the common search for the bearing of the apostolic faith on baptism, eucharist and ministry.

This statement has been written by the Theological Commission of WEF with the purpose of speaking both to the ecumenical community and to those of our own constituency who may belong to churches involved in the ecumenical process, or who more generally seek guidance on how evangelicals should respond to the document.

The WEF is not an organized church nor an organization of churches. It is a fellowship of national and regional evangelical bodies formed with the purpose of encouraging, motivating and enabling the local church to fulfil its scriptural mandate. It represents approximately 100 million Christians around the world. Structurally WEF is polymorphous: it represents about sixty national or regional fellowships, and a variety of denominations, parachurch organizations and individual Christians. The WEF constituency ranges from those who do not observe the sacraments (e.g. Friends) to those for whom sacraments are centrally important to their faith and thought (e.g. some Anglicans and Lutherans). Membership in WEF requires adherence to the Statement of Faith (see Appendix I). Many of the persons who belong to one or other regional national fellowships are members (and leaders) of churches that are also intimately involved in the ecumenical movement. There is, therefore, some overlap of membership.

The WEF is a fellowship of evangelicals. Three characteristics of evangelicals are historically linked to developments in the churches during the last century and a half. The first is a response in the English-speaking world to what was seen as an overemphasis on the sacraments, and to a concomitant devaluation of the need for personal faith in the recipients of the sacraments. This means that evangelicals tend to be 'low church' rather than 'high church' (to use terms current in the Anglican world).

A second characteristic of evangelicals is their stress upon the authority of Scripture and its essential doctrines, such as those enunciated in the Apostles' Creed and the Nicene Creed. We give priority to such matters as the deity of Jesus Christ (in the strict sense of the Councils), the historicity of his virginal conception and bodily resurrection, the substitutionary nature of his atonement, the primacy of justification as the entry-point into a right relationship with God, the necessity of a personal response of faith to the gospel, the exclusive sufficiency of grace as the ground of our salvation and of faith as the means for appropriating it, the prospect of Christ's personal return, and the truthfulness of the divine revelation embodied in Scripture.

Out of this engagement with sacramentalism and theological liberalism, with their resulting de-emphasis on personal faith and on the need for conversion, a third distinctiveness has arisen: evangelicals sense the urgent need to share the good news in worldwide evangelism with those who have not believed in Jesus Christ. Hence our objection to any reduction of the Christian message to a merely social or political gospel and to the idea that there is saving truth in all religions.

In short, emphasis on personal faith rather than the efficacy of the sacraments, acknowledgement of the supreme authority of Scripture above autonomous reason or the traditions of the churches, and the continuing mandate to evangelize the lost, characterize evangelicals today.

From these characteristics it follows that conversion, seen as the turning from sin to God, is for evangelicals the *sine qua non* for fellowship in the body of Christ.

This does not mean that evangelicals have no interest in the sacraments, nor that they hold that Scripture gives ready-made answers to all of life's complex problems, nor that the traditions of the church may be ignored, nor that we may be insensitive to social injustice. It does mean that in responding to BEM we will analyze the issues raised primarily in the light of our perception of God's normative self-disclosure in Scripture.

Amongst evangelicals there is a growing concern about ecclesiological issues and the need to manifest as clearly as possible the visible unity of the body of Christ. We agree, for instance, that:

— The one holy catholic and apostolic church comprises all who call upon the name of the Lord in truth (1 Cor. 1:2) and acknowledge Jesus Christ as Lord (1 Cor. 12:3).
— Membership in this church, the body of Christ, not membership

in any denominational affiliation, constitutes our fundamental identity as people of God.
- The prayerful yearning of our Lord, namely that we experience and display, in truth, that oneness that exists between him and the Father, should be a driving force in our lives (Jn. 17). Visibly to maintain the unity of the Spirit (Eph. 4:3) and to grow into a unity-in-maturity as we strive to attain to the fulness of the stature of Jesus Christ (Eph. 4:16) are constituents in our continuing assignment.
- The visible unity of the church should build upon the truth of the whole gospel.
- In anticipation of the consummation, the Holy Spirit is present in the church, empowering it to live a life worthy of the gospel and to proclaim by word and action the mighty deeds of God who called us out of darkness and into his marvellous light (1 Pet. 2:10).

The WEF Statement of Faith does not contain an article on the church. One reason for this omission is that evangelicals have not generally considered church government, the nature of sacraments and the nature and form of authority in the church to be the most important issues to be faced. Moreover, opinions differ rather widely across the constituency of WEF on the sacraments (or 'ordinances': cf. Appendix II) and church polity. Questions relating to baptism, eucharist and ministry are nevertheless of great interest to evangelicals, though in accordance with our own ecclesiological diversity our evaluations of the BEM proposals vary somewhat.

In this response we will bear in mind the four 'questions' raised by the WCC Commission on Faith and Order (BEM, p. x):

- the extent to which [WEF] can recognize in this text the faith of the Church through the ages;
- the consequences [WEF] can draw from this text for its relations and dialogues with other churches, particularly with those churches which also recognize the text as an expression of the apostolic faith;
- the guidance [WEF] can take from this text for its worship, educational, ethical, and spiritual life and witness;
- the suggestions [WEF] can make for the ongoing work of Faith and Order as it relates the material of this text on Baptism, Eucharist and Ministry to its long-range research project 'Towards the Common Expression of the Apostolic Faith Today'.

We will summarize our response to these questions in the Conclusion.

It is important to note the particular context and origin of the BEM document, made clear in the background and introductory material (see BEM, pp. vii–x; *Churches Respond to BEM* 1 [1986], pop. 1–27; *Ecumenical Perspectives on Baptism, Eucharist and Ministry* [1986], *passim*). The most important point to be considered is that the document is designed to facilitate the process of the union of churches, and therefore it deals with matters which have traditionally hindered this process. Accordingly, it does not set out a fully comprehensive theology of church, ministry and sacraments but deals with areas of difficulty. In many cases these are of a practical and institutional nature, as well as theological and pastoral. Similarly, it seeks to resolve these areas of difficulty by searching for consensus and agreement with a view to establishing grounds for unity where perhaps it had not been anticipated beforehand.

Because of the nature of the WEF and of the origin and history of the BEM document, we cannot respond to the document and the four questions asked of respondents in the same way as denominations and Christian World Communions can, especially those involved directly in the ecumenical process. Nevertheless as members of the body of Christ we express our concern for unity on these issues and therefore submit our observations.

Before dealing with specific points in BEM, there is one major area in which we would offer comment on the document. It concerns the first question about the extent to which we can recognize in this text the faith of the church through the ages. It is one that comes close to the heart of the reason for the existence of the evangelical movement. To facilitate our response, the issue may be formulated as follows: Does the wording of BEM's first question not focus the attention on what is secondary, namely the faith of the church through the ages, rather than on what is primary, that is, the normative witness given in Scripture?

By God's grace, we will approach the BEM document in a spirit of openness and biblical discernment. In dealing with these matters we shall indicate what distinguishes evangelicals from other Christians regarding the issues covered by BEM, and the extent to which our central concerns are reflected in and adopted by BEM.

Baptism

A. Introduction

The framers of the Lima document are to be thanked for their valiant efforts to achieve some measure of unanimity on so disputed a subject as baptism. On this subject our evaluation is so integrally connected with our unity and diversity as evangelicals that a brief explanation seems prudent.

Because the convictions and values that unite WEF constituents (cf. Preamble) do not include a uniform understanding of baptism, the degree of divergence amongst us on this subject is large. Some of us use the term 'regeneration' in connection with baptism (evangelical Lutherans, some Anglicans), others advocate baptism months or years removed from conversion (some Baptists and others), and still others practice no baptism at all (Salvationists, evangelical Friends).

These differences of opinion turn on such issues as the following: the mode of baptism; how baptism is related to faith—whether or not conscious, personal faith must precede baptism (indeed, the precise function of baptism in Christian experience); how those who are baptized are related to the people of God in the Old Testament; and the degree to which baptism should be interpreted as an individual act and the degree to which it should be interpreted corporately. Because of the place of Scripture in evangelical theology, disputes in these areas resolve into disagreements over the meaning of Scripture. We frankly admit that we have not done all we could to bring these disputes to fair debate around the Scriptures, in an effort both to isolate the precise points of our interpretative disagreements and to resolve them.

Nevertheless, most evangelicals would happily subscribe to such points as these: that Christians should be baptized in obedience to God; that baptism is related to the incorporation of people into the church; that baptism implies unity with Christ, and therefore also with Christ's death and resurrection; that it is a symbol or a sign (some would add a 'seal') of that identification; that it is a means of grace, in the sense that by means of baptism God blesses us and gives us assurance; above all, that sacramentalism (cf. Appendix II) must be rejected as unbiblical.

Aspects of the baptism section most evangelicals will appreciate

Among the many features of the Lima document for which most evangelicals will be grateful are the following:

1. The text recognizes the need for conversion and faith (cf. especially B4).

2. The Lima document rightly calls for genuine unity (B2), and insists that the evil divisions based on race, sex and status be transcended. At the same time, it guards against language that might

be taken to call for the abolition of all distinctive *roles* through baptism.

3. The Lima document rightly relegates the mode of baptism to a position of secondary importance. It properly challenges credobaptists, who insist that conscious faith precede baptism, not to be too stringent about the mode; and paedobaptists to recognize that immersion expresses in the best way the Christian's participation in the death and resurrection of Christ.

4. On several fronts, the Baptism section of BEM openly admits the differences of opinion found amongst WCC constituents, even while trying to find points of continuity and agreement. We applaud such frankness, convinced that genuine unity can never be achieved by masking differences.

5. We acknowledge the effort of BEM to grapple with the complex historical and liturgical problems associated with the practice of baptism in relation to the gift of the Spirit, personal faith and the corporate life of the church (B14–23). Its proposals challenge evangelicals to develop their own thinking and practice in this area.

C. Aspects of the baptism section with which evangelicals have difficulty

1. *Sacramental language*: we find we cannot approve the sacramentalist language of the entire section (baptism unites, initiates, gives participation, effects). To be sure, many in the WEF constituency would not feel that the problem lies in the language itself since Reformed theologians have often used similar language. The early Reformers followed the linguistic rule that the sign may stand for the thing signified (i.e. metonymy). Many in the WEF would argue that baptism is not a mere symbol of the grace preceding it, but also an instrument of the grace that it symbolizes (as 'visible word'). The problem, they would argue, is that the sacramental language is not accompanied by an equally firm emphasis on the need for faith, repentance, and conversion, as presuppositions of baptism.

Many WEF constituents would go farther and insist that the clearly sacramentalist language of the Lima document depends far too heavily on church tradition that cannot be traced back to the New Testament itself. Even when conversion and faith properly receive some stress (B4), the clause in question is weakened by being subsumed under an introductory sentence which claims that baptism makes us partakers of the mystery of the death and resurrection of Christ. The same paragraph (B4) goes so far as to say, 'Thus those baptized are pardoned, cleansed and sanctified by Christ, and are given as part of their baptismal experience a new ethical orientation under the guidance of the Holy Spirit.' Again, 'signifies and effects' (B14), implies a sacramentalist causation that few evangelicals could support (though evangelical confessional Lutherans amongst us greatly stress the efficacy of the Word in baptism).

It appears to us that the tensions within the Baptism section of the Lima document are largely confined to sacramentalist controversies (remembering especially the debate on the seal of the Spirit: cf. B14). It is highly significant that the conclusion should be: 'All agree that Christian baptism is in water and the Holy Spirit'. In its context, this statement apparently writes off all non-sacramentalist Christians, who do not tie together water baptism and Holy Spirit baptism as efficacious cause and effect, to say nothing of those who do not practice any baptism (e.g. Salvationists, Friends). In short, most evangelicals will regret the persistently sacramentalist thrust of the entire document.

2. *Use of Scripture*: Many of WEF's constituents would question the baptismal exegesis of BEM (e.g. B2, B3, B4, B5, B6, B8, B9, B10, B19). Amongst the passages quoted are many that do not refer to water-baptism (1 Cor. 12:13 of paramount importance). Most would find considerable difficulty with the appeal BEM makes to Jn. 3:5; 1 Cor. 6:11; Tit. 3:5; Heb. 10:22, to cite but a few examples.

3. *Mere appearance of agreement*: It appears to us that the framers of BEM too frequently use language that is patient of mutually exclusive interpretations. If we are not mistaken in this impression, we must ask whether genuine unity is achieved when each party reads BEM in such a way that the presence of mutually unacceptable opinions is actually hidden.

To take but two examples, all will happily accept the words 'the Lord who bestows his grace upon his people' (B1), but some will worry that the context implies that these words mean God bestows his grace 'at baptism', 'in baptism', or 'in consequence of baptism'. The theological problem at issue is not mere automaticity, for sacramentalist theology strongly maintains the need of faith for *fruitful* reception of the sacraments; it is the problem of a grace-conveying role distinct from that of signification ('visible word'). Again, 'means' in the statement 'Baptism *means* participating in the life, death and resurrection of Jesus Christ' (B3) is ambiguous, for it may refer to the thing signified or to the operation of the rite itself.

Further, silence on some issues may (doubtless unwittingly) convey a greater impression of agreement than is in fact the case. For instance, although the Lima document makes it clear that faith is the required condition for fruitful reception of baptism (B8), and although the Commentary gently takes to task those churches that practice infant baptism 'in an apparently indiscriminate way' (BCom 21), neither makes clear what faith is required. BEM does not rule out the Roman Catholic view that the absence of conscious objection (*obex*) is a sufficient condition for infant regeneration. Most evangelicals, regardless of their views of paedobaptism, would judge such an uncertainty to be a serious liability.

4. *Grounding unity in baptism*: To base unity on the rite of baptism is entirely foreign to Scripture, since 1 Cor. 12:13 does not refer to water-baptism. Biblical unity is based on union with Christ through the Spirit's indwelling (Rom. 8). The full measure of such unity requires agreement in faith; nevertheless our human limitations require that present church unity be based on agreement on the *essentials* of the faith. The rite of baptism is an important issue to the question of union and unity, to the extent that it is related to fellowship with Christ.

BEM's appeal for 'mutual recognition of baptism' (B15, B16) is probably both easier and more difficult within an evangelical framework than within some other traditions. Evangelical distinctives, such as concern for doctrinal truth and the unmasking of merely nominal Christian profession, make the mutual recognition of baptism a difficult matter indeed. Add to this that evangelicals do not agree on the issue of paedobaptism versus credobaptism, any more than do Christians who would not align themselves with the evangelical movement. On the other hand, evangelicals often achieve quite remarkable degrees of unity with other evangelicals at the local level, despite considerable differences in churchmanship. Moreover, a number of evangelical denominations allow individual clergy to follow their own conscience in the matter of baptism, while encouraging them to accept the baptism of quite different traditions. This is possible precisely because for most evangelicals baptism does not loom as large an issue in inter-church cooperation as it does for many others.

5. *The statement on 're-baptism'*: This occurs as the culmination of an historical and theological vignette of the rise and significance of the diverse baptismal practices found within the church today (B11–B13). Although most credobaptists amongst WEF constituents would question the likelihood 'that infant baptism was also practiced in the apostolic age' (B11), the rest of the historical vignette in this section is unobjectionable. However, many statements in B12 seem to becloud the issue (e.g. the faithfulness of Christ as the ground of baptism is not relevant in this particular debate). The distinction 'between those who baptize people at any age and those who baptize only those able to make a confession of faith for themselves' (BCom 12) holds interest, but the real distinction, as we see it, is between

those who baptize only those who do make a confession of faith for themselves, whatever their age, and those who do not. Both positions require similar attitudes to Christian nurture; this point is well taken. Nevertheless, historic credobaptist conviction cannot accept the two positions as 'equivalent alternatives', for the simple reason that credobaptists, to be consistent, normally consider paedobaptism to be no baptism at all.

In BEM (B15, BCom 12), essential disagreements between paedobaptists and credobaptists are treated as if they were differences in emphasis only. In reality, the differences are historic and profound. What is quite clear is that, in the nature of the case, no credobaptist (including the Baptist, Brethren, many free churches, almost all Pentecostalists) can accet the proposition that 'any practice which might be interpreted as "re-baptism" must be avoided' (B13). Credobaptist conviction, by and large, is that re-baptism is a misnomer. The plea in BEM amounts to asking credobaptists to renounce their conviction. By thus writing off more than half of Protestants around the world, BEM becomes needlessly divisive.

Eucharist

A. Introduction

Especially since the sixteenth century, the bread of fellowship has become a major source of discord in Christendom. The framers of the Lima document entered a sensitive area indeed: they deserve our appreciation and their work requires rigorous scrutiny.

Evangelicals differ widely on the importance and the nature of the Lord's Supper. The views range from a minority who do not observe the ordinance at all to those for whom it is an integral part of Christian worship, and from those who consider the Lord's Supper only as a symbolic remembering of Christ's death to those who maintain that Christ is bodily present under the elements of bread and wine. Nevertheless, we would generally agree on the following:

1. that the Lord's Supper commemorates the death of Christ for our sin and points to our communion with Christ in an eternal kingdom;
2. that it is a means by which God blesses and strengthens us, though without spiritual grace being imparted through the physical elements;
3. that participating with faith and a clear conscience is essential;
4. that a sacramentalist understanding of the Lord's Supper should be rejected (cf. Appendix II); and

5. that the understanding of the Lord's Supper as a sacrifice we offer with Christ is unacceptable.

Our concern in this evaluation of the Eucharist section of BEM has been to assess the depth of the agreement reached, to see whether it can accommodate evangelical orientations on faith and church order pertaining to the Lord's Supper, and to evaluate the document in the light of the apostolic teaching of the New Testament.

B. Areas where evangelicals appreciate the eucharist section

Among the emphases for which evangelicals are grateful are the following:

1. The text stresses that the sacrifice of Christ on the cross is unique and unrepeatable (E10).
2. BEM affirms that only through the Holy Spirit is Christ present in the Lord's Supper.
3. The text recognizes communion as 'the meal of the New Covenant—as the anticipation of the Supper of the Lamb' (E1).
4. The section on thanksgiving acknowledges that 'this sacrifice of praise is possible only through Christ' (E4).
5. The Lima document acknowledges that the celebration of holy communion includes the proclamation of the Word—indeed, it is itself an effective proclamation of God's mighty acts and promises (E3, 7, 27).
6. The text affirms that sharing in the Lord's Supper demonstrates the oneness of God's people, and makes plain that personal and social ethical demands are entailed by participation in the eucharist (E19–21).

C. Aspects of the eucharist section with which evangelicals have difficulty

This section reflects rather fully, although in moderate tones, a sacramentalist view, as distinguished from an evangelical one. The word 'eucharist', historically little used in Protestant churches, may already indicate this slant. (We recognize, however, that the term is less important than the substance.)

Sacramentalist emphases are obvious in the following traits:

1. The eucharist is hailed as 'the central act of the Church's worship' (E1) and alluded to in mysteric terms: Christ, as he presides at the meal, is 'the priest who celebrates the mystery of God' (E29).

2. The eucharist is considered the means by which, or the locus in which, the grace of God is actually communicated to the faithful. Although some formulations might be understood in a weaker sense, the repetition of the theme strongly suggests a sacramentalist meaning. This impression is reinforced by the description of the rite as an 'effective sign' (E5—the traditional Roman Catholic definition of a sacrament).

3. The rite is interpreted in terms of 'real presence', a real presence so unique and so closely related to the elements (E13) that it remains a property of the elements after the celebration itself is over (E15). Presumably this view underlies the appeal to respect the practice of the reservation of the elements (E32). BEM refrains from using the term 'transubstantiation' (E13 and ECom 15) but allows the concept within the range of acceptable options, a point implicitly acknowledged by the Commentary ('the deepest reality is the total being of Christ' [ECom 15] states this dogma in non-technical language).

4. The eucharist is emphatically understood as a sacrifice of praise offered to the Father (E3, 4, 23), and as intercession that the church offers not only through Christ but also in communion with Christ (E8). Indeed, after initially and rightly emphasizing that the eucharist is the 'sacrament of the gift which God makes to us in Christ through the power of the Holy Spirit' (E2), BEM's discussion predominantly construes the Lord's Supper in terms of what we offer to God. The *anamnesis* ('memorial') theme is used to justify the idea of a 'representation' beyond 'a calling to mind of what is past and of its significance' (E7): the idea of memorial, we are told, 'refers to this present efficacy of God's work' (E5). At least in the Commentary, the unique and unrepeatable sacrifice of the cross is understood to be 'made actual' (Comm. 8). It is in this context, we are told, that the traditional Roman Catholic designation of the eucharist as 'propitiatory sacrifice' may be understood. This construction is satisfactory neither to traditional Roman Catholics nor to evangelicals.

5. The BEM claim that the world is 'present in the whole eucharist celebration' seems to us to be not only unduly speculative but without Scriptural sanction. The eucharist, we are told, 'is the great sacrifice of praise by which the Church speaks on behalf of the whole creation' (E4, 22, 23).

6. We question whether the need for faith for reception of the rite has received adequate attention in the document. Though one may presume that for BEM, as for the whole Christian tradition, the sacraments are sacraments of faith, it is remarkable that the only reference to faith in the eucharist section of BEM is related to 'discerning the body and blood of Christ' (E13). Most evangelicals believe that

God effectively grants his gift of grace through the Lord's Supper only when the promise of the gospel in the sacrament as the 'visible word' is apprehended by faith. Stressing the necessity of personal faith is a way of honouring the freedom of the Spirit and the purity of justification without works.

In short, BEM's strong sacramentalist emphasis and its relative silence on other views appear to marginalize non-sacramentalist understandings of the Lord's Supper.

D. The Eucharist and the New Testament

It appears to us that extra-biblical (though traditional) developments have been used, consciously or unconsciously, as the hermeneutical key in BEM's study of the New Testament, and this we consider an unfortunate choice. Scripture can play its normative role with respect to the human process of reception and application in the church, only when it interprets itself. By this we do not mean that human interpreters can cut themselves off from their cultural understanding and heritage, but that the unique revelatory status of Scripture must be preserved: in our understanding, Scripture judges all cultures, and not the reverse.

The following points might be mentioned:

1. Though we want to stress that the Lord's Supper is an integral part of what Christians do when they gather together (1 Cor. 11:2), the primary focus on such occasions is the declaration of the Word of God so that God's people may worship him in word and deed: 'Let the word of Christ dwell in you richly as you teach and admonish one another with all wisdom, and as you sing psalms, hymns and spiritual songs with gratitude in your hearts to God' (Col. 3:16; cf. Rom. 12:1–2).

2. Biblical passages on the Lord's Supper offer little warrant for the idea of causal efficacy attributed to the sacrament. Most evangelicals would not apply the words of Jesus in Jn. 6 directly to the eucharistic elements. As to the communication of saving grace, the constant emphasis in the New Testament falls on the mediation of the preached Word of God.

3. Similarly, most evangelicals (but not all) will accept that careful exegesis of the words of institution—'This is my body . . .'—finds no intimation of a change affecting the bread and the wine, apart from the adding of their new function and meaning as signs. To us, the truth of the ascension (Jn. 20:17; Acts 3:21) raises insuperable difficulties with the logic of 'real presence', in the sense of bodily presence.

4. As to sacrificial language, it is strikingly absent from New Testament references to the Lord's Supper. 'Eucharist' (Greek *eucharistia*), to be sure, is a New Testament word for the Christian sacrifice of praise: but it refers to the accompanying prayer, not to the meal itself (1 Cor. 11:24; 14:16). The fact that thanks is offered does not transform the meal into a thank-offering. No clear proof from Scripture may be adduced to support the BEM conception of 'memorial' as 'making present' or 'actual' a past event. Although BEM affirms the unrepeatable nature of Christ's sacrifice (E8), its construction of 'memorial' undermines this affirmation and conflicts with the New Testament emphasis on the once-for-all character of the atonement, set forth, for example, in the Epistle to the Hebrews. Proclamation, yes (1 Cor. 11:26); actualized sacrifice, no.

These biblical considerations on the Lord's Supper must be seen in the context of the evangelical understanding of the gospel. It is centred in Christ's redeeming work on the cross where he died for our sin as our righteous Substitute. On the basis of this work of Christ the Christian church lives, not as an institution that dispenses salvation, but as a community of those who have been justified by grace and who proclaim salvation. Our assessment of BEM's understanding of the Lord's Supper stems therefore from our deep conviction about the essentials of Christian faith.

Ministry

A. An evangelical approach to ministry

In accordance with biblical usage, 'ministry' refers first of all to the varied service by the whole people of God. It consists in the communal or personal communication of the blessings of the gospel. These relate to initial salvation, edification and the meeting of other human needs. As a result of this service or ministry, its recipients become aware of God's presence and power and more attuned to his will and purpose.

The term 'the ministry' (or 'minister') may be used to refer to the officially appointed ministers working within a reasonably structured situation. The purpose of the 'appointed ministers' is to equip others for the work of ministry (Eph. 4:11–13). One should not infer, however, that effective ministry is in any way restricted to this group of people as they function in formal situations. Nor is it to be supposed that by virtue of such membership or appointment members of this group possess any permanent character or qualities. The key dynamic is God working in the 'ministers' (official or unofficial) to enable them to become channels of his gracious presence.

The ways in which the officially appointed ministry is exercised are many. These are not restricted to any set list, but range from personal testimony to all kinds of serving relationships. The titles that may be given to formally appointed, official ministers vary, often according to the type of activity in which they are involved. Such names include bishop, pastor, elder, deacon, evangelist, missionary, preacher, counsellor. These are primarily functional terms rather than being indicative of status. Official appointment (which may be known as 'ordination' or 'induction' or 'commissioning' or 'setting apart') implies recognition of a God-given ministry. While such appointment may confer certain authority within the group making the appointment (and those in fellowship with it), this authority is conditional upon continued exercise of faithful ministry. Such formal appointment or ordination is not *necessary* for ministry.

The qualities required in a person for fruitful ministry include prior gifting by God, spiritual sensitivity and maturity, trust in and obedience to God. Normally such ministry cannot be exercised without a sense of divine calling and an obedient response. Faithfulness and fruitfulness in ministry depend on obedience to the guidance of God and on the continual blessing of God. Such ministry calls for acknowledgement and intercession on the part of those whom it serves.

These are, in brief, some of the distinguishing features of the concept of ministry held by most evangelicals. Many evangelical churches exhibit these features in whole or in part and consider them to be biblical, rather than simply denominational or historical.

It is to be noted that some issues treated as basic in the BEM report (such as 'validity' and 'apostolic succession') are also important in an evangelical approach to church and ministry. Nevertheless, we deal with them in ways so different from BEM, and so commonly express them in other terminology, that they are hardly recognized as the same issues. It is therefore difficult for us to comment directly on those parts of BEM that touch on these particular technical terms; the underlying issues themselves need to be identified and discussed. It is at this fundamental level that WEF wishes to interact with the BEM section on ministry.

Specific comments

1. *The calling of the whole people of God (M1–6)*
In general, the first six paragraphs of the Ministry section of BEM set

out a valid framework for considering the question of Christian ministry, with their focus on the sinful state of humankind, the redemptive work of Christ, and the calling of the people of God through the Spirit. We applaud the fact that reflection on ministry is set within the context of the question, 'How, according to the will of God and under the guidance of the Holy Spirit, is the life of the Church to be understood and ordered, so that the Gospel may be spread and the community built up in love?' (M6).

Given the significant differences amongst Christians 'in their understanding of how the life of the Church is to be ordered' and especially of 'the place and forms of the ordained ministry' (M6), it is understandable that the theme of ordained ministry should have been singled out for special consideration. Nevertheless, it is a pity that, in seeking to answer the fundamental question about the way the church is to be ordered, the Lima document largely fails to capitalize on the excellent foundation laid in M1–6. Instead, it largely restricts its discussion to the traditional patterns of ordained professional clergy. By focusing its attention on this topic, BEM has perpetuated the problem by defining church unity in the narrow terms of the nature and role of the ordained clergy, rather than placing it in the broader context of the ministry of 'the whole people of God'.

2. The church and the ordained ministry (M7–18) and ordination (M39–55)

While the observation that 'the church has never been without persons holding specific authority and responsibility' (M9) is unobjectionable, BEM's understanding of the nature and role of such ministry presents serious problems. We will deal with the following: the constitutive role ascribed to the ministry of official clergy; the designation of a particular form of ministry as priestly; the sacramental understanding of ordination; the notion of the ordained ministry as the focus of unity; the ordination of women.

First, we find it incompatible with the New Testament to claim that the ordained ministry, or the service of persons who are 'publicly and continually responsible' for the church, is 'constitutive for the life and witness of the church' (M8). Rather, the church is constituted by the presence of the resurrected Christ through the Holy Spirit in the believing community (Mt. 18:20; 28:16–20), the members of which minister as the priestly people of God to one another and to the world. The ordained ministers can be validly described as 'representatives of Jesus Christ to the community' (M11), as long as it is clear that they represent Christ in a way that is not *essentially* different from the way in which any believer is called and gifted to represent Christ.

Second, evangelicals query the suggestion that presidency of the eucharistic celebration might legitimate calling ministers 'priests' (M17); they would not find in the metaphorical language of Rom. 15:16 a warrant for a ministerial priesthood distinct from the priesthood of all believers (cf. 1 Pet. 2:10).

Third, undoubtedly the ordained minister can be—and often has been—a 'focus of unity'. Normally ministers are qualified to guide the Christian community according to God's Word, and it is the duty of the members to follow this guidance. The moral authority of the minister and his loyalty in expounding the Scripture are an important force to keep the church united in the bond of peace. But the ordained ministry in itself is not a guarantee against strife and division; indeed, the ordained ministry can be the source of such strife. And it must also be said that unity has often been reached or maintained at the cost of serious doctrinal deviations.

Fourth, reservations must be expressed when BEM claims that in the rite of ordination the authority of Jesus Christ is conferred on the minister (M15). From the biblical point of view the problematic nature of such conferral is compounded by the sacramental understanding of ordination elaborated in M39–50. Though BEM stresses the importance of the involvement of the congregation, the invocation of the power of the Spirit and the commitment of the ordinand (M41–44), ordination is still said to be 'a sign performed in faith that the spiritual relationship signified is present in, with and through the words spoken, the gestures made and the forms employed' (M43).

Fifth, considering ordination as conferring this special status also compounds the difficulties for some churches in regard to the role of women in ministry. It is therefore not surprising that BEM offers no solution to the controversy over this matter, but simply expresses the need for further study of the issue. But the theological problems are considerably simplified if ordination is seen as public recognition by the church of a call to exercise a spiritual gift for ministry and the commitment of the church to the support of the gifted person in the exercise of his or her ministry. In this case, 'male-ness' or 'female-ness' is not the primary issue, but gift and calling. Amongst evangelicals the question is whether or how the constraints on certain types of ministries in the New Testament (e.g. 1 Tim 2:12) apply today.

3. *The forms of the ordained ministry (M19–33) and succession in the apostolic tradition (M34–38)*

BEM suggests that 'the threefold ministry of bishop, presbyter and deacon may serve today as an expression of the unity we seek and also as a means for achieving it' (M22). Yet BEM makes this proposal despite its acknowledgement that no such precedence can be established from the New Testament (M19, 22), that the form of the threefold pattern itself has changed remarkably over the centuries, and that currently it 'stands evidently in need of reform' (M24). The only reason given for recommending the threefold ministry as an expression of unity or as a means for achieving it is that of historical development. For an evangelical this is clearly insufficient warrant. Why should the contemporary church be narrower in its understanding of ministry than the New Testament, where we find a variety of forms of ministry (cf. M19)? To press for a specific, hierarchical form of 'threefold ministry' is to turn a legitimate diversity into a divisive issue. Thus BEM's commendation of the threefold ministry achieves the opposite of what is intended.

Historical development is also taken as the basis for a particular understanding of the apostolic succession. It is argued that the succession of bishops' became one of the ways . . . in which the apostolic tradition of the Church was expressed' (M36). Accordingly, it is claimed that non-episcopal churches should see the virtue of the episcopacy, especially when it is recognized that 'the reality and function of the episcopal ministry have been preserved in many of these churches' without the use of the word 'bishop' (M37). 'Apostolic tradition' is understood as 'continuity with the apostles and their proclamation' and 'continuity in the permanent characteristics of the Church of the apostles' (M34), such as witness and proclamation of the gospel, fellowship, service and worship. If apostolic tradition were to be understood in this sense only, then the primacy ascribed to 'apostolic tradition' would mean the acknowledgement of Scripture as critical norm over all subsequent tradition, a position to which evangelicals subscribe. But in BEM 'apostolic tradition' also refers to the extended tradition handed down and preserved by the churches in unbroken episcopal succession. In that case, the normative Scriptures become subservient to the church tradition.

Most evangelicals feel that the plea BEM makes for episcopacy as a preferable model of church government is hardly convincing. For one thing, BEM itself acknowledges that it may be a 'sign' but is not a 'guarantee' of the 'continuity and unity of the Church' (M38). Furthermore, it grants that other forms of ministry have been able to maintain biblical Christianity in its spiritual power (M33, 37). No biblical reason is offered for regarding episcopacy (in whatever form it may appear) as having any inherent superiority. BEM also fails to mention that 'bishop' and 'elder' are used interchangeably in the New Testament. It seems, therefore, that BEM simply justifies an existing practice. (*viz.* episcopacy), rather than subjecting it to the biblical norm and assessing its ability to serve 'adequately . . . the proclamation of the apostolic faith' today (M35).

Evangelicals can indeed endorse the view that a 'uniform answer' to the question of the precise functions and titles of those in ministry 'is not required for the mutual recognition of the ordained ministry' (M28). It is helpful for practical and administrative reasons to set out some general guidelines for the functions of the different ministers for bishops, presbyters and deacons (M29–31). Evangelicals, however, want to place more emphasis upon the 'variety of charisms' in 'the community which lives in the power of the Spirit' (M32). Ways must certainly be found to prevent 'the ordained ministry, which is itself a charism', from becoming 'a hindrance' to the other charisms and the enrichment of the church's life which the Spirit wills through them. We have strong reservations about the notion of the bishop or other ordained person signifying the personal presence of Christ among his people; we rejoice that BEM places appropriate emphasis on the 'personal, collegial and communal' manner in which ministry gifts are to be exercised (M26–27).

4. *Towards the mutual recognition of the ordained ministries (M52–55)*

Since evangelicals find it difficult to restrict ministry to the ordained and, in any case, find problems with the idea of sacramental ordination within the apostolic succession and with a separate order of priesthood, the question of mutual recognition of ministry must be seen in a larger perspective than is outlined in M51-55.

Respect for history and even desire for greater church unity, of which universal episcopacy would be a sign, do not seem to be sufficient motives for adopting the 'threefold ministry'. What is important is that churches live 'in faithful continuity with the apostolic faith and mission [and] have a ministry of Word and sacrament' (M53). Most evangelicals will doubt that episcopacy such as BEM tends to favour really belongs to the well-being of the church, let alone to its *esse* (being). Rather than inviting non-episcopal churches 'to recover the sign of episcopal succession' (M53b), we would encourage all churches to rediscover, both in theory and in practice, the exercise of various gifts by the members in the body, as the ministry of all to all.

Similarly, mutual recognition of ministries at the local level often takes place without formal ecclesiastical agreement. This is evident, for example, amongst evangelicals when the service of preachers, evangelists, Bible teachers and counsellors from other communions is warmly welcomed. Though we are humbled by our fragmentation and lack of official mutual recognition of ministry and sacraments, nevertheless significant unity is 'publicly manifest' (M53) by the fellowship that exists within such situations. The value of such God-given ministry is demonstrated by its fruitfulness in the lives of those who receive it.

Conclusion

In light of the foregoing considerations, brief answers to the four questions put to the readers of the Lima document by its authors (p. x) may be offered:

1. We confess that, although the church in its long history has often been unfaithful to the Lord, the Lord has remained faithful to the church and has not withdrawn his Holy Spirit from his people. We agree that valuable lessons can be learned from ecclesiastical tradition. We are somewhat disquieted, however, that the suggested standard for measuring BEM and our own traditions is 'the faith of the Church through the ages' and not the Holy Scriptures themselves. For the most part, the WEF constituency would gladly recognize the applicability of many individual statements in the Lima document to their own churches; virtually all would find difficulty subscribing to the whole, primarily because of the emphasis on sacramentalism which most of us find unwarranted by Scripture.

2. Since most evangelicals will find it difficult to identify in the Lima document an adequate 'expression of the apostolic faith', the set question as it is cast becomes irrelevant. The thrust of the question, however, invites us to examine our own commitments and beliefs afresh and to renew our own doctrines of baptism, the Lord's Supper and ministry in the light of the Scriptures. Since WEF is a fellowship of national evangelical alliances and other evangelicals, it is not in a position to instruct its members how to engage in conversation with other ecclesiastical groups. Yet the presence of serious differences regarding baptism, the Lord's Supper and ministry among Christian communions is an incentive to us to bring our understanding of Scripture to bear in the dialogue with other communions.

3. Because our perspective on the authority of Scripture, the nature of salvation, the role of the church, and the means of grace differs from the prevailing views of BEM, evangelicals are less likely than some others to use the Lima document for guidance in matters of worship and witness. Those amongst us, however, who have tended to underestimate the importance and value of the Lord's Supper should be encouraged to review their theology and practice.

4. We wish to encourage Faith and Order in its endeavour to focus on the substance of the faith as the basis for true unity. We pray therefore that the long-range project 'Towards the Common Expression of the Apostolic Faith Today' will serve to that end. We make two suggestions:

   a. that in the quest for unity in faith, the Scriptures function as supreme norm, and that traditions, including our own, be regarded as *interpretative* traditions—themselves subject to Scripture;

b. that in this project Faith and Order take into account more carefully the convictions of the millions of active believers who live and serve Christ in the context of a non-sacramentalist understanding of Christianity.

At the same time, we frankly acknowledge that the failure of Faith and Order to do so in the past has in part stemmed from our failure to make our views known clearly, charitably and persistently. We would like to think that this response will contribute something to that end.

Appendix I
World Evangelical Fellowship Statement of Faith

We believe in the *Holy Scriptures* as originally given by God, divinely inspired, infallible, entirely trustworthy; and the supreme authority in all matters of faith and conduct;

One God, eternally existent in three persons, Father, Son, and Holy Spirit;

Our *Lord Jesus Christ*, God manifest in the flesh, His virgin birth, His sinless human life, His divine miracles, His vicarious and atoning death, His bodily resurrection, His ascension, His mediatorial work, and His personal return in power and glory;

The *Salvation* of lost and sinful man through the shed blood of the Lord Jesus Christ by faith apart from works, and regeneration by the Holy Spirit;

The *Holy Spirit*, by whose indwelling the believer is enabled to live a holy life, to witness and work for the Lord Jesus Christ;

The *Unity of the Spirit* of all true believers, the Church, the Body of Christ;

The *Resurrection* of both the saved and the lost; them that are saved unto the resurrection of life, them that are lost unto the resurrection of damnation.

Appendix II
Mystery, Sacrament, Ordinance

Part of the contemporary debate on baptism, eucharist and ministry lies hidden behind the terminology. Indeed, the stance of many evangelicals cannot easily be understood apart from an appreciation of some terminological developments during the earliest centuries of the Christian era.

Although the term 'sacrament' does not appear in BEM until B23, in the eyes of most readers of all persuasions, evangelicals included, the approach toward baptism, eucharist and ministry in this document is evidently 'sacramentalist'. Unfortunately, 'sacrament' and 'sacramentalist' have diverse meanings for different speakers and writers. Some review of the rise and the use of the terms therefore seems advisable.

In contemporary evangelicalism, some define 'sacrament' as a religious rite instituted by Jesus Christ. With so simple a definition, few would find theological difficulty. Even credobaptists (i.e. those who believe that only those who articulate their own faith should be baptized) would not find fault with the first known application of the term to baptism, found in Pliny's letters. Writing to Trajan, Pliny describes what he has learned from apostate Christians of early Christian faith and practice:

> . . . they had met regularly before dawn on a fixed day to chant verses alternately among themselves in honour of Christ as if to a god, *and also to bind themselves by oath* [Lat. *dicere secum invicem seque sacramento*], not for any criminal purpose, but to abstain from theft . . . (Letters X.xcvi.7)

Scholars usually recognize that 'oath' (*sacramentum*) refers to baptismal vows.

The history of the church shows that from this earliest usage three linguistic developments contributed to the contemporary situation.

First, the Greek term *mystērion* ('mystery' in older English versions of the New Testament, often 'secret' in more recent versions) was applied to the Lord's Supper and to baptism, even though no such use is found in the New Testament. The word designated in common parlance the secret ceremonies which lay at the heart of various 'mystery-religions', as they are called for that very reason; the central rites were thought to mediate divine benefits. The mystery-religions were forms of devotion warmer and more personal than the official exercises of city and imperial religion. Because they had a considerable appeal throughout the Roman Empire in the first centuries of our era, contacts with Christianity were inevitable. Superficial similarities between the mystery-rites and the church's baptism and holy supper made it an easy step to transfer the term *mystērion* to the Christian observances.

Second, an effort was then made to relate this new usage to the teaching of the New Testament. The argument was one of analogy: just as miracles and signs are the visible manifestation of the powerful presence of the *mystery* of the kingdom (Mk. 4:11 par.), just as Jesus' physical body is the visible demonstration of the *mystery* of the Word made flesh (1 Tim. 3:16), and just as the church is the bodily manifestation of Christ, expressing the *mystery* of the relationship between Christ and the church (Eph. 5:32), so also the bread and wine are the visible manifestations of the presence of Christ in the Lord's Supper—and therefore another 'mystery'. That link is not made in the New Testament, where *mystērion* almost exclusively refers to divine revelation in some measure hidden in previous ages but now revealed in the coming and teaching of Jesus Christ and his Spirit-anointed disciples.

Third, the Greek word *mystērion* was translated into Latin by the term *sacramentum*, from which our word 'sacrament' derives. The Latin *sacramentum* meant 'a thing set apart as sacred' and, more specifically, referred to 'a military oath of obedience as administered by the commander'. In the latter sense, it had been used very early for Christian baptism, as we have seen in Pliny's quotation, in harmony with the popular simile of the church as the 'militia of Christ'. As the rendering for *mystērion*, however, 'sacrament' took over the connotations of the Greek word, and the idea of ritual efficacy, for salvation and blessings, attached to it. That was reinforced by the association with sacredness. Later generations within the Roman Catholic and Orthodox branches of the church not only elevated the sacraments to a place of prominence in the church's worship, but increasingly stressed that sacraments are efficacious signs, conveying the grace that they contain, and that grace is communicated by virtue of the rite.

Since this view, which may be called sacramentalism, lacks biblical support, it is rejected by most evangelicals. Because of its connotations some of them studiously avoid the use of the word 'sacrament' itself; they rather speak of 'ordinances', i.e. things which the Lord has ordained.

The Lima Document: Text

I. The Institution of Baptism

1. Christian baptism is rooted in the ministry of Jesus of Nazareth, in his death and in his resurrection. It is incorporation into Christ, who is the crucified and risen Lord; it is entry into the New Covenant between God and God's people. Baptism is a gift of God, and is administered in the name of the Father, the Son, and the Holy Spirit. St Matthew records that the risen Lord, when sending his disciples into the world, commanded them to baptize (Matt. 28:18–20). The univer-

sal practice of baptism by the apostolic Church from its earliest days is attested in letters of the New Testament, the Acts of the Apostles, and the writings of the Fathers. The churches today continue this practice as a rite of commitment to the Lord who bestows his grace upon his people.

II. The Meaning of Baptism

2. Baptism is the sign of new life through Jesus Christ. It unites the one baptized with Christ and with his people. The New Testament scriptures and the liturgy of the Church unfold the meaning of baptism in various images which express the riches of Christ and the gifts of his salvation. These images are sometimes linked with the symbolic uses of water in the Old Testament. Baptism is participation in Christ's death and resurrection (Rom. 6:3–5; Col. 2:12); a washing away of sin (I Cor. 6:11); a new birth (John 3:5); an enlightenment by Christ (Eph. 5:14); a reclothing in Christ (Gal. 3:27); a renewal by the Spirit (Titus 3:5); the experience of salvation from the flood (I Peter 3:20–21); an exodus from bondage (I Cor. 10:1–2) and a liberation into a new humanity in which barriers of division whether of sex or race or social status are transcended (Gal. 3:27–28; I Cor. 12:13). The images are many but the reality is one.

A. Participation in Christ's Death and Resurrection

3. Baptism means participating in the life, death and resurrection of Jesus Christ. Jesus went down into the river Jordan and was baptized in solidarity with sinners in order to fulfil all righteousness (Matt. 3:15). This baptism led Jesus along the way of the Suffering Servant, made manifest in his sufferings, death and resurrection (Mark 10:38–40, 45). By baptism, Christians are immersed in the liberating death of Christ where their sins are buried, where the 'old Adam' is crucified with Christ, and where the power of sin is broken. Thus those baptized are no longer slaves to sin, but free. Fully identified with the death of Christ, they are buried with him and are raised here and now to a new life in the power of the resurrection of Jesus Christ, confident that they will also ultimately be one with him in a resurrection like his (Rom. 6:3–11; Col. 2:13, 3:1; Eph. 2:5–6).

B. Conversion, Pardoning and Cleansing

4. The baptism which makes Christians partakers of the mystery of Christ's death and resurrection implies confession of sin and conver-

sion of heart. The baptism administered by John was itself a baptism of repentance for the forgiveness of sins (Mark 1:4). The New Testament underlines the ethical implications of baptism by representing it as an ablution which washes the body with pure water, a cleansing of the heart of all sin, and an act of justification (Heb. 10:22; I Peter 3:21; Acts 22:16; I Cor. 6:11). Thus those baptized are pardoned, cleansed and sanctified by Christ, and are given as part of their baptismal experience a new ethical orientation under the guidance of the Holy Spirit.

C. The Gift of the Spirit

5. The Holy Spirit is at work in the lives of people before, in and after their baptism. It is the same Spirit who revealed Jesus as the Son (Mark 1:10–11) and who empowered and united the disciples at Pentecost (Acts 2). God bestows upon all baptized persons the anointing and the promise of the Holy Spirit, marks them with a seal and implants in their hearts the first instalment of their inheritance as sons and daughters of God. The Holy Spirit nurtures the life of faith in their hearts until the final deliverance when they will enter into its full possession, to the praise of the glory of God (II Cor. 1:21–22; Eph. 1:13–14).

D. Incorporation into the Body of Christ

6. Administered in obedience to our Lord, baptism is a sign and seal of our common discipleship. Through baptism, Christians are brought into union with Christ, with each other and with the Church of every time and place. Our common baptism, which unites us to Christ in faith, is thus a basic bond of unity. We are one people and are called to confess and serve one Lord in each place and in all the world. The union with Christ which we share through baptism has important implications for Christian unity. 'There is . . . one baptism, one God and Father of us all . . .' (Eph. 4:4–6). When baptismal unity is realized in one holy, catholic, apostolic Church, a genuine Christian witness can be made to the healing and reconciling love of God. Therefore, our one baptism into Christ constitutes a call to the churches to overcome their divisions and visibly manifest their fellowship.

E. The Sign of the Kingdom

7. Baptism initiates the reality of the new life given in the midst of the

present world. It gives participation in the community of the Holy Spirit. It is a sign of the Kingdom of God and of the life of the world to come. Through the gifts of faith, hope and love, baptism has a dynamic which embraces the whole of life, extends to all nations, and anticipates the day when every tongue will confess that Jesus Christ is Lord to the glory of God the Father.

III. Baptism and Faith

8. Baptism is both God's gift and our human response to that gift. It looks towards a growth into the measure of the stature of the fullness of Christ (Eph. 4:13). The necessity of faith for the reception of the salvation embodied and set forth in baptism is acknowledged by all churches. Personal commitment is necessary for responsible membership in the body of Christ.

9. Baptism is related not only to momentary experience, but to lifelong growth into Christ. Those baptized are called upon to reflect the glory of the Lord as they are transformed by the power of the Holy Spirit, into his likeness, with ever increasing splendour (II Cor. 3:18). The life of the Christian is necessarily one of continuing struggle yet also of continuing experience of grace. In this new relationship, the baptized live for the sake of Christ, of his Church and of the world which he loves, while they wait in hope for the manifestation of God's new creation and for the time when God will be all in all (Rom. 8:18–24; I Cor. 15:22–28, 49–57).

10. As they grow in the Christian life of faith, baptized believers demonstrate that humanity can be regenerated and liberated. They have a common responsibility, here and now, to bear witness together to the Gospel of Christ, the Liberator of all human beings. The context of this common witness is the Church and the world. Within a fellowship of witness and service, Christians discover the full significance of the one baptism as the gift of God to all God's people. Likewise, they acknowledge that baptism, as a baptism into Christ's death, has ethical implications which not only call for personal sanctification, but also motivate Christians to strive for the realization of the will of God in all realms of life (Rom. 6:9ff; Gal. 3:27–28; I Peter 2:21–4:6).

IV. Baptismal Practice

A. Baptism of Believers and Infants

11. While the possibility that infant baptism was also practised in the apostolic age cannot be excluded, baptism upon personal profession

of faith is the most clearly attested pattern in the New Testament documents.

In the course of history, the practice of baptism has developed in a variety of forms. Some churches baptize infants brought by parents or guardians who are ready, in and with the Church, to bring up the children in the Christian faith. Other churches practise exclusively the baptism of believers who are able to make a personal confession of faith. Some of these churches encourage infants or children to be presented and blessed in a service which usually involves thanksgiving for the gift of the child and also the commitment of the mother and father to Christian parenthood.

All churches baptize believers coming from other religions or from unbelief who accept the Christian faith and participate in catechetical instruction.

12. Both the baptism of believers and the baptism of infants take place in the Church as the community of faith. When one who can answer for himself or herself is baptized, a personal confession of faith will be an integral part of the baptismal service. When an infant is baptized, the personal response will be offered at a later moment in life. In both cases, the baptized person will have to grow in the understanding of faith. For those baptized upon their own confession of faith, in there is always the constant requirement of a continuing growth of personal response in faith. In the case of infants, personal confession is expected later, and Christian nurture is directed to the eliciting of this confession. All baptism is rooted in and declares Christ's faithfulness unto death. It has its setting within the life and faith of the Church and, through the witness of the whole Church, points to the faithfulness of God, the ground of all life in faith. At every baptism the whole congregation reaffirms its faith in God and pledges itself to provide an environment of witness and service. Baptism should, therefore, always be celebrated and developed in the setting of the Christian community.

13. Baptism is an unrepeatable act. Any practice which might be interpreted as 're-baptism' must be avoided.

B. Baptism—Chrismation—Confirmation

14. In God's work of salvation, the paschal mystery of Christ's death and resurrection is inseparably linked with the pentecostal gift of the Holy Spirit. Similarly, participation in Christ's death and resurrection is inseparably linked with the receiving of the Spirit. Baptism in its full meaning signifies and effects both.

Christians differ in their understanding as to where the sign of the gift of the Spirit is to be found. Different actions have become associated with the giving of the Spirit. For some it is the water rite itself. For others, it is the anointing with chrism and/or the imposition of hands, which many churches call confirmation. For still others it is all three, as they see the Spirit operative throughout the rite. All agree that Christian baptism is in water and the Holy Spirit.

C. Towards Mutual Recognition of Baptism

15. Churches are increasingly recognizing one another's baptism as the one baptism into Christ when Jesus Christ has been confessed as Lord by the candidate or, in the case of infant baptism, when confession has been made by the church (parents, guardians, godparents and congregation) and affirmed later by personal faith and commitment. Mutual recognition of baptism is acknowledged as an important sign and means of expressing the baptismal unity given in Christ. Wherever possible, mutual recognition should be expressed explicitly by the churches.

16. In order to overcome their differences, believer baptists and those who practise infant baptism should reconsider certain aspects of their practices. The first may seek to express more visibly the fact that children are placed under the protection of God's grace. The latter must guard themselves against the practice of apparently indiscriminate baptism and take more seriously their responsibility for the nurture of baptized children to mature commitment to Christ.

V. The Celebration of Baptism

17. Baptism is administered with water in the name of the Father, the Son and the Holy Spirit.

18. In the celebration of baptism the symbolic dimension of water should be taken seriously and not minimalized. The act of immersion can vividly express the reality that in baptism the Christian participates in the death, burial and resurrection of Christ.

19. As was the case in the early centuries, the gift of the Spirit in baptism may be signified in additional ways; for example, by the sign of the laying on of hands, and by anointing or chrismation. The very sign of the cross recalls the promised gift of the Holy Spirit who is the instalment and pledge of what is yet to come when God has fully redeemed those whom he has made his own (Eph. 1:13–14). The recovery of such vivid signs may be expected to enrich the liturgy.

20. Within any comprehensive order of baptism at least the following elements should find a place: the proclamation of the scriptures

referring to baptism; an invocation of the Holy Spirit; a renunciation of evil; a profession of faith in Christ and the Holy Trinity; the use of water; a declaration that the persons baptized have acquired a new identity as sons and daughters of God, and as members of the Church, called to be witnesses of the Gospel. Some churches consider that Christian initiation is not complete without the sealing of the baptized with the gift of the Holy Spirit and participation in holy communion.

21. It is appropriate to explain in the context of the baptismal service the meaning of baptism as it appears from scriptures (i.e. the participation in Christ's death and resurrection, conversion, pardoning and cleansing, gift of the Spirit, incorporation into the body of Christ and sign of the Kingdom).

22. Baptism is normally administered by an ordained minister, though in certain circumstances others are allowed to baptize.

23. Since baptism is intimately connected with the corporate life and worship of the Church, it should normally be administered during public worship, so that the members of the congregation may be reminded of their own baptism and may welcome into their fellowship those who are baptized and whom they are committed to nurture in the Christian faith. The sacrament is appropriate to great festival occasions such as Easter, Pentecost and Epiphany, as was the practice in the early Church.

Commentary (6)

The inability of the churches mutually to recognize their various practices of baptism as sharing in the one baptism, and their actual dividedness in spite of mutual baptismal recognition, have given dramatic visibility to the broken witness of the Church. The readiness of the churches in some places and times to allow differences of sex, race, or social status to divide the body of Christ has further called into question genuine baptismal unity of the Christian community (Gal. 3:27–28) and has seriously compromised its witness. The need to recover baptismal unity is at the heart of the ecumenical task as it is central for the realization of genuine partnership within the Christian communities.

Commentary (12)

When the expressions 'infant baptism' and 'believers' baptism' are used, it is necessary to keep in mind that the real distinction is between those who baptize people at any age and those who baptize only those able to make a confession of faith for themselves. The differences between infant and believers' baptism become less sharp when it is recognized that both forms of baptism embody God's own initiative in Christ and express a response of faith made within the believing community.

The practice of infant baptism emphasizes the corporate faith and the faith which the child shares with its parents. The infant is born into a broken world and shares in its brokenness. Through baptism, the promise and claim of the Gospel are laid upon the child. The personal faith of the recipient of baptism and faithful participation in the life of the Church are essential for the full fruit of baptism.

The practice of believers' baptism emphasizes the explicit confession of the person who responds to the grace of God in and through the community of faith and who seeks baptism.

Both forms of baptism require a similar and responsible attitude towards Christian nurture. A rediscovery of the continuing character of Christian nurture may facilitate the mutual acceptance of different initiation practices.

In some churches which unite both infant-baptist and believer-baptist traditions, it has been possible to regard as equivalent alternatives for entry into the Church both a pattern whereby baptism follows upon a presentation and blessing in infancy. This example invites other churches to decide whether they, too, could not recognize equivalent alternatives in their reciprocal relationships and in church union negotiations.

Commentary (13)

Churches which have insisted on a particular form of baptism or which have had serious questions about the authenticity of other churches' sacraments and ministries have at times required persons coming from other church traditions to be baptized before being received into full communicant membership. As the churches come to fuller mutual understanding and acceptance of one another and enter into closer relationships in witness and service, they will want to refrain from any practice which might call into question the sacramental integrity of other churches or which might diminish the unrepeatability of the sacrament of baptism.

Commentary (14)

(a) Within some traditions it is explained that as baptism conforms us to Christ crucified, buried and risen, so through chrismation Christians receive the gift of the pentecostal Spirit from the anointed Son.

(b) If baptism, as incorporation into the body of Christ, points by its very nature to the eucharistic sharing of Christ's body and blood, the question arises as to how a further and separate rite an be interposed between baptism and admission to communion. Those churches which baptize children but refuse them a share in the eucharist before such a rite may wish to ponder whether they have fully appreciated and accepted the consequences of baptism.

(c) Baptism needs to be constantly reaffirmed. The most obvious form of such reaffirmation is the celebration of the paschal mystery or during the baptism of others.

Commentary (18)

As seen in some theological traditions, the use of water, with all its positive associations with life and blessing, signifies the continuity between the old and the new creation, thus revealing the significance of baptism not only for human beings but also for the whole cosmos. At the same time, the use of water represents a purification of creation, a dying to that which is negative and destructive in the world: those who are baptized into the body of Christ are made partakers of a renewed existence.

Commentary (21)

Recent discussion indicates that more attention should be given to misunderstandings encouraged by the socio-cultural context in which baptism takes place.

(a) In some parts of the world, the giving of a name in the baptismal liturgy has led to confusion between baptism and customs surrounding name-giving. This confusion is especially harmful if, in cultures predominantly not Christian, the baptized are required to assume Christian names not rooted in their cultural tradition. In making regulations for baptism, churches should be careful to keep the emphasis on the true Christian significance of baptism and to avoid unnecessarily alienating the baptized from their local culture through the imposition of foreign names. A name which is inherited from one's original culture roots the baptized in that culture, and at the same time manifests the universality of baptism, incorporation into the one Church, holy, catholic and apostolic, which stretches over all the nations of the earth.

(b) In many large European and North American majority churches infant baptism is often practised in an apparently indiscriminate way. This contributes to the reluctance of churches which practise believer's baptism to acknowledge the validity of infant baptism; this fact should lead to more critical reflection on the meaning of baptism within those majority churches themselves.

(c) Some African churches practise baptism of the Holy Spirit without water, through the laying on of hands, while recognizing other churches' baptism. A study is required concerning this practice and its relation to baptism with water.

Eucharist

I. The Institution of the Eucharist

1. The Church receives the eucharist as a gift from the Lord. St Paul wrote: 'I have received from the Lord what I also delivered to you, that the Lord Jesus on the night when he was betrayed took bread, and when he had given thanks, he broke it, and said: "This is my body, which is for you. Do this in remembrance (*anamnesis*) of me." In the same way also the cup, after supper, saying: "This cup is the new covenant in my blood. Do this, as often as you drink it, in remembrance of me.' " (I Cor. 11:23–25; cf. Matt. 26:26–29; Mark 14:22–25; Luke 22:14–20).

The meals which Jesus is recorded as sharing during his earthly ministry proclaim and enact the nearness of the Kingdom, of which the feeding of the multitudes is a sign. In his last meal, the fellowship of the Kingdom was connected with the imminence of Jesus' suffering. After his resurrection, the Lord made his presence known to his disciples in the breaking of the bread. Thus the eucharist continues these meals of Jesus during his earthly life and after his resurrection, always as a sign of the Kingdom. Christians see the eucharist prefigured in the Passover memorial of Israel's deliverance from the land of bondage and in the meal of the Covenant on Mount Sinai (Ex. 24). It is the new paschal meal of the Church, the meal of the New Covenant, which Christ gave to his disciples as the *anamnesis* of his death and resurrection, as the anticipation of the Supper of the Lamb (Rev. 19:9). Christ commanded his disciples thus to remember and encounter him in this sacramental meal, as the continuing people of God, until his return. The last meal celebrated by Jesus was a liturgical meal employing symbolic words and actions. Consequently the eucharist is a sacramental meal which by visible signs communicates to us God's love in Jesus Christ, the love by which Jesus loved his own 'to the end' (John 13:1). It has acquired many names: for example, the Lord's Supper, the breaking of bread, the holy communion, the divine liturgy, the mass. Its celebration continues as the central act of the Church's worship.

II. The Meaning of the Eucharist

2. The eucharist is essentially the sacrament of the gift which God makes to us in Christ through the power of the Holy Spirit. Every Christian receives this gift of salvation through communion in the body and blood of Christ. In the eucharistic meal, in the eating and drinking of the bread and wine, Christ grants communion with himself. God himself acts, giving life to the body of Christ and renewing each member. In accordance with Christ's promise, each baptized member of the body of Christ receives in the eucharist the assurance of the forgiveness of sins (Matt. 26:28) and the pledge of eternal life (John 6:51–58). Although the eucharist is essentially one complete act, it will be considered here under the following aspects: thanksgiving to the Father, memorial of Christ, invocation of the Spirit, communion of the faithful, meal of the Kingdom.

A. The Eucharist as Thanksgiving to the Father

3. The eucharist, which always includes both word and sacrament, is a proclamation and a celebration of the work of God. It is the great thanksgiving to the Father for everything accomplished in creation, redemption and sanctification, for everything accomplished by God now in the Church and in the world in spite of the sins of human beings, for everything that God will accomplish in bringing the Kingdom to fulfilment. Thus the eucharist is the benediction (*berakah*) by which the Church expresses its thankfulness for all God's benefits.
4. The eucharist is the great sacrifice of praise by which the Church speaks on behalf of the whole creation. For the world which God has reconciled is present at every eucharist: in the bread and wine, in the persons of the faithful, and in the prayers they offer for themselves and for all people. Christ unites the faithful with himself and includes their prayers within his own intercession so that the faithful are transfigured and their prayers accepted. This sacrifice of praise is possible only through Christ, with him and in him. The bread and wine, fruits of the earth and of human labour, are presented to the Father in faith and thanksgiving. The eucharist thus signifies what the world is to become: an offering and hymn of praise to the Creator, a universal communion

in the body of Christ, a kingdom of justice, love and peace in the Holy Spirit.

B. The Eucharist as Anamnesis or Memorial of Christ

5. The eucharist is the memorial of the crucified and risen Christ, i.e. the living and effective sign of his sacrifice, accomplished once and for all on the cross and still operative on behalf of all humankind. The biblical idea of memorial as applied to the eucharist refers to this present efficacy of God's work when it is celebrated by God's people in a liturgy.

6. Christ himself with all that he has accomplished for us and for all creation (in his incarnation, servant-hood, ministry, teaching, suffering, sacrifice, resurrection, ascension and sending of the Spirit) is present in this *anamnesis*, granting us communion with himself. The eucharist is also the foretaste of his *parousia* and of the final kingdom.

7. The *anamnesis* in which Christ acts through the joyful celebration of his Church is thus both representation and anticipation. It is not only a calling to mind of what is past and of its significance. It is the Church's effective proclamation of God's mighty acts and promises.

8. Representation and anticipation are expressed in thanksgiving and intercession. The Church, gratefully recalling God's mighty acts of redemption, beseeches God to give the benefits of these acts to every human being. In thanksgiving and intercession, the Church is united with the Son, its great High Priest and Intercessor (Rom. 8:34; Heb. 7:25). The eucharist is the sacrament of the unique sacrifice of Christ, who ever lives to make intercession for us. It is the memorial of all that God has done for the salvation of the world. What it was God's will to accomplish in the incarnation, life, death, resurrection and ascension of Christ, God does not repeat. These events are unique and can neither be repeated nor prolonged. In the memorial of the eucharist, however, the Church offers its intercession in communion with Christ, our great High Priest.

9. The *anamnesis* of Christ is the basis and source of all Christian prayer. So our prayer relies upon and is united with the continual intercession of the risen Lord. In the eucharist, Christ empowers us to live with him, to suffer with him and to pray through him as justified sinners, joyfully and freely fulfilling his will.

10. In Christ we offer ourselves as a living and holy sacrifice in our daily lives (Rom. 12:1; I Peter 2:5); this spiritual worship, acceptable to God, is nourished in the eucharist, in which we are sanctified and reconciled in love, in order to be servants of reconciliation in the world.

11. United to our Lord and in communion with all the saints and martyrs, we are renewed in the covenant sealed by the blood of Christ.

12. Since the *anamnesis* of Christ is the very content of the preached Word as it is of the eucharistic meal, each reinforces the other. The celebration of the eucharist properly includes the proclamation of the Word.

13. The words and acts of Christ at the institution of the eucharist stand at the heart of the celebration; the eucharistic meal is the sacrament of the body and blood of Christ, the sacrament of his real presence. Christ fulfils in a variety of ways his promise to be always with his own even to the end of the world. But Christ's mode of presence in the eucharist is unique. Jesus said over the bread and wine of the eucharist: 'This is my body . . . this is my blood . . .' What Christ declared is true, and this truth is fulfilled every time the eucharist is celebrated. The Church confesses Christ's real, living and active presence in the eucharist. While Christ's real presence in the eucharist does not depend on the faith of the individual, all agree that to discern the body and blood of Christ, faith is required.

C. The Eucharist as Invocation of the Spirit

14. The Spirit makes the crucified and risen Christ really present to us in the eucharistic meal, fulfilling the promise contained in the words of institution. The presence of Christ is clearly the centre of the eucharist, and the promise contained in the words of institution is therefore fundamental to the celebration. Yet it is the Father who is the primary origin and final fulfilment of the eucharistic event. The incarnate Son of God by and in whom it is accomplished is its living centre. The Holy Spirit is the immeasurable strength of love which makes it possible and continues to make it effective. The bond between the eucharistic celebration and the mystery of the Triune God reveals the role of the Holy Spirit as that of the One who makes the historical words of Jesus present and alive. Being assured by Jesus' promise in the words of institution that it will be answered, the Church prays to the Father for the gift of the Holy Spirit in order that the eucharistic event may be a reality: the real presence of the crucified and risen Christ giving his life for all humanity.

15. It is in virtue of the living word of Christ and by the power of the Holy Spirit that the bread and wine become the sacramental signs of Christ's body and blood. They remain so for the purpose of communion.

16. The whole action of the eucharist has an 'epikletic' character

because it depends upon the work of the Holy Spirit. In the words of the liturgy, this aspect of the eucharist finds varied expression.

17. The Church, as the community of the new covenant, confidently invokes the Spirit, in order that it may be sanctified and renewed, led into all justice, truth and unity, and empowered to fulfil its mission in the world.

18. The Holy Spirit through the eucharist gives a foretaste of the Kingdom of God: the Church receives the life of the new creation and the assurance of the Lord's return.

D. The Eucharist as Communion of the Faithful

19. The eucharistic communion with Christ who nourishes the life of the Church is at the same time communion within the body of Christ which is the Church. The sharing in one bread and the common cup in a given place demonstrates and effects the oneness of the sharers with Christ and with their fellow sharers in all times and places. It is in the eucharist that the community of God's people is fully manifested. Eucharistic celebrations always have to do with the whole Church, and the whole Church is involved in each local eucharistic celebration. In so far as a church claims to be a manifestation of the whole Church, it will take care to order its own life in ways which take seriously the interests and concerns of other churches.

20. The eucharist embraces all aspects of life. It is a representative act of thanksgiving and offering on behalf of the whole world. The eucharistic celebration demands reconciliation and sharing among all those regarded as brothers and sisters in the one family of God and is a constant challenge in the search for appropriate relationships in social, economic and political life (Matt. 5:23f; I Cor. 10:16f; I Cor. 11:20–22; Gal. 3:28). All kinds of injustice, racism, separation and lack of freedom are radically challenged when we share in the body and blood of Christ. Through the eucharist the all-renewing grace of God penetrates and restores human personality and dignity. The eucharist involves the believer in the central event of the world's history. As participants in the eucharist, therefore, we prove inconsistent if we are not actively participating in this ongoing restoration of the world's situation and the human condition. The eucharist shows us that our behaviour is inconsistent in face of the reconciling presence of God in human history: we are placed under continual judgment by the persistence of unjust relationships of all kinds in our society, the manifold divisions on account of human pride, material interest and power politics and, above all, the obstinacy of unjustifiable confessional oppositions within the body of Christ.

21. Solidarity in the eucharistic communion of the body of Christ and responsible care of Christians for one another and the world find specific expression in the liturgies: in the mutual forgiveness of sins; the sign of peace; intercession for all; the eating and drinking together; the taking of the elements to the sick and those in prison or the celebration of the eucharist with them. All these manifestations of love in the eucharist are directly related to Christ's own testimony as a servant, in whose servanthood Christians themselves participate. As God in Christ has entered into the human situation, so eucharistic liturgy is near to the concrete and particular situations of men and women. In the early Church the ministry of deacons and deaconesses gave expression in a special way to this aspect of the eucharist. The place of such ministry between the table and the needy properly testifies to the redeeming presence of Christ in the world.

E. The Eucharist as Meal of the Kingdom

22. The eucharist opens up the vision of the divine rule which has been promised as the final renewal of creation, and is a foretaste of it. Signs of this renewal are present in the world wherever the grace of God is manifest and human beings work for justice, love and peace. The eucharist is the feast at which the Church gives thanks to God for these signs and joyfully celebrates and anticipates the coming of the Kingdom in Christ (I Cor. 11:26; Matt. 26:29).

23. The world, to which renewal is promised, is present in the whole eucharistic celebration. The world is present in the thanksgiving to the Father, where the Church speaks on behalf of the whole creation; in the memorial of Christ, where the Church, united with its great High Priest and Intercessor, prays for the world; in the prayer for the gift of the Holy Spirit, where the Church asks for sanctification and new creation.

24. Reconciled in the eucharist, the members of the body of Christ are called to be servants of reconciliation among men and women and witnesses of the joy of resurrection. As Jesus went out to publicans and sinners and had table-fellowship with them during his earthly ministry, so Christians are called in the eucharist to be in solidarity with the outcast and to become signs of the love of Christ who lived and sacrificed himself for all and now gives himself in the eucharist.

25. The very celebration of the eucharist is an instance of the Church's participation in God's mission to the world. This participation takes everyday form in the proclamation of the Gospel, service of the neighbour, and faithful presence in the world.

26. As it is entirely the gift of God, the eucharist brings in to the

present age a new reality which transforms Christians into the image of Christ and therefore makes them his effective witnesses. The eucharist is precious food for missionaries, bread and wine for pilgrims on their apostolic journey. The eucharistic community is nourished and strengthened for confessing by word and action the Lord Jesus Christ who gave his life for the salvation of the world. As it becomes one people, sharing the meal of the one Lord, the eucharistic assembly must be concerned for gathering also those who are at present beyond its visible limits, because Christ invited to his feast all for whom he died. Insofar as Christians cannot unite in full fellowship around the same table to eat the same loaf and drink from the same cup, their missionary witness is weakened at both the individual and the corporate levels.

III. The Celebration of the Eucharist

27. The eucharistic liturgy is essentially a single whole, consisting historically of the following elements in varying sequence and of diverse importance:

- hymns of praise;
- act of repentance;
- declaration of pardon;
- proclamation of the Word of God, in various forms;
- confession of faith (creed);
- intercession for the whole Church and for the world;
- preparation of the bread and wine;
- thanksgiving to the Father for the marvels of creation, redemption and sanctification (deriving from the Jewish tradition of the *berakah*);
- the words of Christ's institution of the sacrament according to the New Testament tradition;
- the *anamnesis* or memorial of the great acts of redemption, passion, death, resurrection, ascension and Pentecost, which brought the Church into being;
- the invocation of the Holy Spirit (*epiklesis*) on the community, and the elements of bread and wine (either before the words of institution or after the memorial, or both; or some other reference to the Holy Spirit which adequately expresses the 'epikletic' character of the eucharist);
- consecration of the faithful to God;
- reference to the communion of saints;
- prayer for the return of the Lord and the definitive manifestation of his Kingdom;

- the Amen of the whole community;
- the Lord's prayer;
- sign of reconciliation and peace;
- the breaking of the bread;
- eating and drinking in communion with Christ and with each member of the Church;
- final act of praise;
- blessing and sending.

28. The best way towards unity in eucharistic celebration and communion is the renewal of the eucharistic celebration and communion is the renewal of the eucharist itself in the different churches in regard to teaching and liturgy. The churches should test their liturgies in the light of the eucharistic agreement now in the process of attainment.

The liturgical reform movement has brought the churches closer together in the manner of celebrating the Lord's Supper. However, a certain liturgical diversity compatible with our common eucharistic faith is recognized as a healthy and enriching fact. The affirmation of a common eucharistic faith does not imply uniformity in either liturgy or practice.

29. In the celebration of the eucharist, Christ gathers, teaches and nourishes the Church. It is Christ who invites to the meal and who presides at it. He is the shepherd who leads the people of God, the prophet who announces the Word of God, the priest who celebrates the mystery of God. In most churches, this presidency is signified by an ordained minister. The one who presides at the eucharistic celebration in the name of Christ makes clear that the rite is not the assemblies' own creation or possession; the eucharist is received as a gift from Christ living in his Church. The minister of the eucharist is the ambassador who represents the divine initiative and expresses the connection of the local community with other local communities in the universal Church.

30. Christian faith is deepened by the celebration of the Lord's Supper. Hence the eucharist should be celebrated frequently. Many differences of theology, liturgy and practice are connected with the varying frequency with which the Holy Communion is celebrated.

31. As the eucharist celebrates the resurrection of Christ, it is appropriate that it should take place at least every Sunday. As it is the new sacramental meal of the people of God, every Christian should be encouraged to receive communion frequently.

32. Some churches stress that Christ's presence in the consecrated elements continues after the celebration. Others place the main emphasis on the act of celebration itself and on the consumption of

the elements in the act of communion. The way in which the elements are treated requires special attention. Regarding the practice of reserving the elements, each church should respect the practices and piety of the others. Given the diversity in practice among the churches and at the same time taking note of the present situation in the convergence process, it is worthwhile to suggest:

- that, on the one hand, it be remembered, especially in sermons and instruction, that the primary intention of reserving the elements is their distribution among the sick and those who are absent, and
- on the other hand, it be recognized that the best way of showing respect for the elements served in the eucharistic celebration is by their consumption, without excluding their use for communion of the sick.

33. The increased mutual understanding expressed in the present statement may allow some churches to attain a greater measure of eucharistic communion among themselves and so bring closer the day when Christ's divided people will be visibly reunited around the Lord's Table.

Commentary (8)

It is in the light of the significance of the eucharist as intercession that references to the eucharist in Catholic theology as 'propitiatory sacrifice' may be understood. The understanding is that there is only one expiation, that of the unique sacrifice of the cross, made actual in the eucharist and presented before the Father in the intercession of Christ and of the Church for all humanity.

In the light of the biblical conception of memorial, all churches might want to review the old controversies about 'sacrifice' and deepen their understanding of the reasons why other traditions than their own have either used or rejected this term.

Commentary (13)

Many churches believe that by the words of Jesus and by the power of the Holy Spirit, the bread and wine of the eucharist become, in a real though mysterious manner, the body and blood of the risen Christ, i.e., of the living Christ present in all his fullness. Under the signs of bread and wine, the deepest reality is the total being of Christ who comes to us in order to feed us and transform our entire being. Some other churches, while affirming a real presence of Christ at the eucharist, do not link that presence so definitely with the signs of bread and wine. The decision remains for the churches whether this difference can be accommodated within the convergence formulated in the text itself.

Commentary (14)

This is not to spiritualize the eucharistic presence of Christ but to affirm the indissoluble union between the Son and the Spirit. This union makes it clear that the eucharist is not a magical or mechanical action but a prayer addressed to the Father, one which emphasizes the Church's utter dependence. There is an intrinsic relationship between the words of institution, Christ's promise, and the epiklesis, *the invocation of the Spirit, in the liturgy. The* epiklesis, *in relation to the words of institution is located differently in various liturgical traditions. In the early liturgies the whole 'prayer action' was thought of as bringing about the reality promised by Christ. The invocation of the Spirit was made both on the community and on the elements of bread and wine. Recovery of such an understanding may help us overcome our difficulties concerning a special moment of consecration.*

Commentary (15)

In the history of the Church there have been various attempts to understand the mystery of the real and unique presence of Christ in the eucharist. Some are content merely to affirm this presence without seeking to explain it. Others consider it necessary to assert a change wrought by the Holy Spirit and Christ's words, in consequence of which there is no longer just ordinary bread and wine but the body and blood of Christ. Others again have developed an explanation of the real presence which, though not claiming to exhaust the significance of the mystery, seeks to protect it from damaging interpretations.

Commentary (19)

Since the earliest days, baptism has been understood as the sacrament by which believers are incorporated into the body of Christ and are endowed with the Holy Spirit. As long as the right of the baptized believers and their ministers to participate in and preside over eucharistic celebration in one church is called into question by those who preside over and are members of other eucharistic congregations, the catholicity of the eucharist is less manifest. There is discussion in many churches today about the inclusion of baptized children as communicants at the Lord's Supper.

Commentary (28)

Since New Testament days, the church has attached the greatest importance to the continued use of the elements of bread and wine which Jesus used at the Last Supper. In certain parts of the world, where bread and wine are not customary or obtainable, it is now sometimes held that local food and drink serve better to anchor the eucharist in everyday life. Further study is required concerning the question of which features of the Lord's Supper were unchangeably instituted by Jesus, and which features remain within the Church's competence to decide.

Ministry

I. The Calling of the Whole People of God

1. In a broken world God calls the whole of humanity to become God's people. For this purpose God chose Israel and then spoke in a unique and decisive way in Jesus Christ, God's Son. Jesus made his own nature, condition and cause of the whole human race, giving himself as a sacrifice for all. Jesus' life of service, his death and resurrection, are the foundation of a new community which is built up continually by the good news of the Gospel and the gifts of the sacraments. The Holy Spirit unites in a single body those who follow Jesus Christ and sends them as witnesses into the world. Belonging to the Church means living in communion with God through Jesus Christ in the Holy Spirit.

2. The life of the Church is based on Christ's victory over the powers of evil and death, accomplished once for all. Christ offers forgiveness, invites to repentance and delivers from destruction. Through Christ, people are enabled to turn in praise to God and in service to their neighbours. In Christ they find the source of new life in freedom, mutual forgiveness and love. Through Christ their hearts and minds are directed to the consummation of the Kingdom where Christ's victory will become manifest and all things made new. God's

purpose is that, in Jesus Christ, all people should share in this fellowship.

3. The Church lives through the liberating and renewing power of the Holy Spirit. That the Holy Spirit was upon Jesus is evidenced in his baptism, and after the resurrection that same Spirit was given to those who believed in the Risen Lord in order to recreate them as the body of Christ. The Spirit calls people to faith, sanctifies them through many gifts, gives them strength to witness to the Gospel, and empowers them to serve in hope and love. The Spirit keeps the Church in the truth and guides it despite the frailty of its members.

4. The Church is called to proclaim and prefigure the Kingdom of God. It accomplishes this by announcing the Gospel to the world and by its very existence as life the body of Christ. In Jesus the Kingdom of God came among us. He offered salvation to sinners. He preached good news to the poor, release to the captives, recovery of sight to the blind, liberation to the oppressed (Luke 4:18). Christ established a new access to the Father. Living in this communion with God, all members of the Church are called to confess their faith and to give account of their hope. They are to identify with the joys and sufferings of all people as they seek to witness in caring love. The members of Christ's body are to struggle with the oppressed towards that freedom and dignity promised with the coming of the Kingdom. This mission needs to be carried out in varying political, social and cultural contexts. In order to fulfil this mission faithfully, they will seek relevant forms of witness and service in each situation. In so doing they bring to the world a foretaste of the joy and glory of God's Kingdom.

5. The Holy Spirit bestows on the community diverse and complementary gifts. These are for the common good of the whole people and are manifested in acts of service within the community and to the world. They may be gifts of communicating the Gospel in word and deed, gifts of healing, gifts of praying, gifts of teaching and learning, gifts of serving, gifts of guiding and following, gifts of inspiration and vision. All members are called to discover, with the help of the community, the gifts they have received and to use them for the building up of the Church and for the service of the world to which the Church is sent.

6. Though the churches are agreed in their general understanding of the calling of the people of God, they differ in their understanding of how the life of the Church is to be ordered. In particular, there are differences concerning the place and forms of the ordained ministry. As they engage in the effort to overcome these differences, the churches need to work from the perspective of the calling of the whole people of God. A common answer needs to be found to the following

question: How, according to the will of God and under the guidance of the Holy Spirit, is the life of the Church to be understood and ordered, so that the Gospel may be spread and the community built up in love?

II. The Church and the Ordained Ministry

7. Differences in terminology are part of the matter under debate. In order to avoid confusion in the discussions on the ordained ministry in the Church, it is necessary to delineate clearly how various terms are used in the following paragraphs.

a) The word *charism* denotes the gifts bestowed by the Holy Spirit on any member of the body of Christ for the building up of the community and the fulfilment of its calling.
b) The word *ministry* in its broadest sense denotes the service to which the whole people of God is called, whether as individuals, as a local community, or as the universal Church. Ministry or ministries can also denote the particular institutional forms which this service may take.
c) The term *ordained ministry* refers to persons who have received a charism and whom the church appoints for service by ordination through the invocation of the Spirit and the laying on of hands.
d) Many churches use the word *priest* to denote certain ordained ministers. Because this usage is not universal, this document will discuss the substantive questions in paragraph 17.

A. The Ordained Ministry

8. In order to fulfil its mission, the Church needs persons who are publicly and continually responsible for pointing to its fundamental dependence on Jesus Christ, and thereby provide, within a multiplicity of gifts, a focus of its unity. The ministry of such persons, who since very early times have been ordained, is constitutive for the life and witness of the Church.

9. The Church has never been without persons holding specific authority and responsibility. Jesus chose and sent the disciples to be witnesses of the Kingdom (Matt. 10:1–8). The Twelve were promised that they would 'sit on thrones judging the tribes of Israel' (Luke 22:30). A particular role is attributed to the Twelve within the communities of the first generation. They are witnesses of the Lord's life and resurrection (Acts 1:21–26). They lead the community in prayer, teaching, the breaking of bread, proclamation and service

(Acts 2:42–47; 6:2–6, etc.). The very existence of the Twelve and other apostles shows that, from the beginning, there were differentiated roles in the community.

10. Jesus called the Twelve to be representatives of the renewed Israel. At that moment they represent the whole people of God and at the same time exercise a special role in the midst of that community. After the resurrection they are among the leaders of the community. It can be said that the apostles prefigure both the Church as a whole and the persons within it who are entrusted with the specific authority and responsibility. The role of the apostles as witnesses to the resurrection of Christ is unique and unrepeatable. There is therefore a difference between the apostles and the ordained ministers whose ministries are founded on theirs.

11. As Christ chose and sent the apostles, Christ continues through the Holy Spirit to choose and call persons into the ordained ministry. As heralds and ambassadors, ordained ministers are representatives of Jesus Christ to the community, and proclaim his message of reconciliation. As leaders and teachers they call the community to submit to the authority of Jesus Christ, the teacher and prophet, in whom law and prophets were fulfilled. As pastors, under Jesus Christ the chief shepherd, they assemble and guide the dispersed people of God, in anticipation of the coming Kingdom.

12. All members of the believing community, ordained and lay, are interrelated. On the one hand, the community needs ordained ministers. Their presence reminds the community of the divine initiative, and of the dependence of the Church on Jesus Christ, who is the source of its mission and the foundation of its unity. They serve to build up the community in Christ and to strengthen its witness. In them the Church seeks an example of holiness and loving concern. On the other hand, the ordained ministry has no existence apart from the community. Ordained ministers can fulfil their calling only in and for the community. They cannot dispense with the recognition, the support and the encouragement of the community.

13. The chief responsibility of the ordained ministry is to assemble and build up the body of Christ by proclaiming and teaching the Word of God, by celebrating the sacraments, and by guiding the life of the community in its worship, its mission and its caring ministry.

14. It is especially in the eucharistic celebration that the ordained ministry is the visible focus of the deep and all-embracing communion between Christ and the members of his body. In the celebration of the eucharist, Christ gathers, teaches and nourishes the Church. It is Christ who invites to the meal and who presides at it. In most churches this presidency is signified and represented by an ordained minister.

B. Ordained Ministry and Authority

15. The authority of the ordained minister is rooted in Jesus Christ, who has received it from the Father (Matt. 28:18), and who confers it by the Holy Spirit through the act of ordination. This act takes place within a community which accords public recognition to a particular person. Because Jesus came as one who serves (Mark 10:45; Luke 22:27), to be set apart means to be consecrated to service. Since ordination is essentially a setting apart with prayer for the gift of the Holy Spirit, the authority of the ordained ministry is not to be understood as the possession of the ordained person but as a gift for the continuing edification of the body in and for which the minister has been ordained. Authority has the character of responsibility before God and is exercised with the cooperation of the whole community.

16. Therefore, ordained ministers must not be autocrats or impersonal functionaries. Although called to exercise wise and loving leadership on the basis of the Word of God, they are bound to the faithful in interdependence and reciprocity. Only when they seek the response and acknowledgment of the community can their authority be protected from the distortions of isolation and domination. They manifest and exercise the authority of Christ in the way Christ himself revealed God's authority to the world, by committing their life to the community. Christ's authority is unique. 'He spoke as one who has authority (*exousia*), not as the scribes' (Matt. 7:29). This authority is an authority governed by love for the 'sheep who have no shepherd' (Matt. 9:36). It is confirmed by his life of service and, supremely, by his death and resurrection. Authority in the Church can only be authentic as it seeks to conform to this model.

C. Ordained Ministry and Priesthood

17. Jesus Christ is the unique priest of the new covenant. Christ's life was given as a sacrifice for all. Derivatively, the Church as a whole can be described as a priesthood. All members are called to offer their being 'as a living sacrifice' and to intercede for the Church and the salvation of the world. Ordained ministers are related, as are all Christians, both to the priesthood of Christ, and to the priesthood of the Church. But they may appropriately be called priests because they fulfil a particular priestly service by strengthening and building up the royal and prophetic priesthood of the faithful through word and sacraments, through their prayers of intercession, and through their pastoral guidance of the community.

D. The Ministry of Men and Women in the Church

18. Where Christ is present, human barriers are being broken. The Church is called to convey to the world the image of a new humanity. There is in Christ no male or female (Gal. 3:28). Both women and men must discover together their contributions to the service of Christ in the Church. The Church must discover the ministry which can be provided by women as well as that which can be provided by men. A deeper understanding of the comprehensiveness of ministry which reflects the interdependence of men and women needs to be more widely manifested in the life of the Church.

Though they agree on this need, the churches draw different conclusions as to the admission of women to the ordained ministry. An increasing number of churches have decided that there is no biblical or theological reason against ordaining women, and many of them have subsequently proceeded to do so. Yet many churches hold that the tradition of the Church in this regard must not be changed.

III. The Forms of the Ordained Ministry

A. Bishops, Presbyters and Deacons

19. The New Testament does not describe a single pattern of ministry which might serve as a blueprint or continuing norm for all future ministry in the Church. In the New Testament there appears rather a variety of forms which existed at different places and times. As the Holy Spirit continued to lead the Church in life, worship and mission, certain elements from this early variety were further developed and became settled into a more universal pattern of ministry. During the second and third centuries, a threefold pattern of bishop, presbyter and deacon became established as the pattern of ordained ministry throughout the Church. In succeeding centuries, the ministry by bishop, presbyter and deacon underwent considerable changes in its practical exercise. At some points of crisis in the history of the Church, the continuing functions of ministry were in some places and communities distributed according to structures other than the predominant threefold pattern. Sometimes appeal was made to the New Testament in justification of these other patterns. In other cases, the restructuring of ministry was held to lie within the competence of the Church as it adapted to changed circumstances.

20. It is important to be aware of the changes the threefold ministry has undergone in the history of the Church. In the earliest instances, where threefold ministry is mentioned, the reference is to the local

eucharistic community. The bishop was the leader of the community. He was ordained and installed to proclaim the Word and preside over the celebration of the eucharist. He was surrounded by a college of presbyters and by deacons who assisted in his tasks. In this context the bishop's ministry was a focus of unity within the whole community.

21. Soon, however, the functions were modified. Bishops began increasingly to exercise *episkopé* over several local communities at the same time. In the first generation, apostles had exercised *episkopé* in the wider Church. Later Timothy and Titus are recorded to have fulfilled a function of *episkopé* in a given area. Later again this apostolic task is carried out in a new way by the bishops. They provide a focus for unity in life and witness within areas comprising several eucharistic communities. As a consequence, presbyters and deacons are assigned new roles. The presbyters become the leaders of the local eucharistic community, and as assistants of the bishops, deacons receive responsibilities in the larger area.

22. Although there is no single New Testament pattern, although the Spirit has many times led the Church to adapt its ministries to contextual needs, and although other forms of the ordained ministry have been blessed with the gifts of the Holy Spirit, nevertheless the threefold ministry of bishop, presbyter and deacon may serve today as an expression of the unity we seek and also as a means for achieving it. Historically, it is true to say, the threefold ministry became the generally accepted pattern in the Church of the early centuries and is still retained today by many churches. In the fulfilment of their mission and service the churches need people who in different ways express and perform the tasks of the ordained ministry in its diaconal, presbyteral and episcopal aspects and functions.

23. The Church as the body of Christ and the eschatological people of God is constituted by the Holy Spirit through a diversity of gifts or ministries. Among these gifts a ministry of *episkopé* is necessary to express and safeguard the unity of the body. Every church needs this ministry of unity in some form in order to be the Church of God, the one body of Christ, a sign of the unity of all in the Kingdom.

24. The threefold pattern stands evidently in need of reform. In some churches the collegial dimension of leadership in the eucharistic community has suffered diminution. In others, the function of deacons has been reduced to an assistant role in the celebration of the liturgy: they have ceased to fulfil any function with regard to the diaconal witness of the Church. In general, the relation of the presbyterate to the episcopal ministry has been discussed throughout the centuries, and the degree of the presbyter's participation in the episcopal ministry is still for many an unresolved question of far-reaching ecumenical

importance. In some cases, churches which have not formally kept the threefold form have, in fact, maintained certain of its original patterns.

25. The traditional threefold pattern thus raises questions for all the churches. Churches maintaining the threefold pattern will need to ask how its potential can be fully developed for the most effective witness of the Church in this world. In this task churches not having the threefold pattern should also participate. They will further need to ask themselves whether the threefold pattern as developed does not have a powerful claim to be accepted by them.

B. Guiding Principles for the Exercise of the Ordained Ministry in the Church

26. Three considerations are important in this respect. The ordained ministry should be exercised in a personal, collegial and communal way. It should be *personal* because the presence of Christ among his people can most effectively be pointed to by the person ordained to proclaim the Gospel and to call the community to serve the Lord in unity of life and witness. It should also be *collegial*, for there is need for a college of ordained ministers sharing in the common task of representing the concerns of the community. Finally, the intimate relationship between the ordained ministry and the community should find expression in a *communal* dimension where the exercise of the ordained ministry is rooted in the life of the community and requires the community's effective participation in the discovery of God's will and the guidance of the Spirit.

27. The ordained ministry needs to be constitutionally or canonically ordered and exercised in the Church in such a way that each of these three dimensions can find adequate expression. At the level of the local eucharistic community there is need for an ordained minister acting within a collegial body. Strong emphasis should be placed on the active participation of all members in the life and the decision-making of the community. At the regional level there is again need for an ordained minister exercising a service of unity. The collegial and communal dimensions will find expression in regular representative synodal gatherings.

C. Functions of Bishops, Presbyters and Deacons

28. What can then be said about the functions and even the titles of bishops, presbyters and deacons? A uniform answer to this question is not required for the mutual recognition of the ordained ministry. The

following considerations on functions are, however, offered in a tentative way.

29. *Bishops* preach the Word, preside at the sacraments, and administer discipline in such a way as to be representative pastoral ministers of oversight, continuity and unity in the Church. They have pastoral oversight of the area to which they are called. They serve the apostolicity and unity of the Church's teaching, worship and sacramental life. They have responsibility for leadership in the Church's mission. They relate the Christian community in their area to the wider Church, and the universal Church to their community. They, in communion with the presbyters and deacons and the whole community, are responsible for the orderly transfer of ministerial authority in the Church.

30. *Presbyters* serve as pastoral ministers of the Word and at the sacraments in a local eucharistic community. They are preachers and teachers of the faith, exercise pastoral care, and bear responsibility for the discipline of the congregation to the end that the world may believe and that the entire membership of the Church may be renewed, strengthened and equipped in ministry. Presbyters have particular responsibility for the preparation of members for Christian life and ministry.

31. *Deacons* represent to the Church its calling as servant in the world. By struggling in Christ's name with the myriad needs of societies and persons, deacons exemplify the interdependence of worship and service in the Church's life. They exercise responsibility in the worship of the congregation: for example by reading the scriptures, preaching and leading the people in prayer. They help in the teaching of the congregation. They exercise a ministry of love within the community. They fulfil certain administrative tasks and may be elected to responsibilities for governance.

D. Variety of Charisms

32. The community which lives in the power of the Spirit will be characterized by a variety of charisms. The Spirit is the giver of diverse gifts which enrich the life of the community. In order to enhance their effectiveness, the community will recognize publicly certain of these charisms. While some serve permanent needs in the life of the community, others will be temporary. Men and women in the communities of religious orders fulfil a service which is of particular importance for the life of the Church. The ordained ministry, which is itself a charism, must not become a hindrance for the variety of these charisms. On the contrary, it will help the community to

discover the gifts bestowed on it by the Holy Spirit and will equip members of the body to serve in a variety of ways.

33. In the history of the Church there have been times when the truth of the Gospel could only be preserved through prophetic and charismatic leaders. Often new impulses could find their way into the life of the Church only in unusual ways. At times reforms required a special ministry. The ordained ministers and the whole community will need to be attentive to the challenge of such special ministries.

IV. Succession in the Apostolic Tradition

A. Apostolic Tradition in the Church

34. In the Creed, the Church confesses itself to be apostolic. The Church lives in continuity with the apostles and their proclamation. The same Lord who sent the apostles continues to be present in the Church. The Spirit keeps the Church in the apostolic tradition until the fulfilment of history in the Kingdom of God. Apostolic tradition in the Church means continuity in the permanent characteristics of the Church of the apostles: witness to the apostolic faith, proclamation and fresh interpretation of the Gospel, celebration of baptism and the eucharist, the transmission of ministerial responsibilities, communion in prayer, love, joy and suffering, service to the sick and the needy, unity among the local churches and sharing the gifts which the Lord has given to each.

B. Succession of the Apostolic Ministry

35. The primary manifestation of apostolic succession is to be found in the apostolic tradition of the Church as a whole. The succession is an expression of the permanence and, therefore, of the continuity of Christ's own mission in which the Church participates. Within the Church the ordained ministry has a particular task of preserving and actualizing the apostolic faith. The orderly transmission of the ordained ministry is therefore a powerful expression of the continuity of the Church throughout history; it also underlines the calling of the ordained minister as guardian of the faith. Where churches see little importance in orderly transmission, they should ask Jesus themselves whether they have not to change their conception of continuity in the apostolic tradition. On the other hand, where the ordained ministry does not adequately serve the proclamation of the apostolic faith, churches must ask themselves whether their ministerial structures are not in need of reform.

36. Under the particular historical circumstances of the growing Church in the early centuries, the succession of bishops became one of the ways, together with the transmission of the Gospel and the life of the community, in which the apostolic tradition of the Church was expressed. This succession was understood as serving, symbolizing and guarding the continuity of the apostolic faith and communion.

37. In churches which practise the succession through the episcopate, it is increasingly recognized that a continuity in apostolic faith, worship and mission has been preserved in churches which have not retained the form of historic episcopate. This recognition finds additional support in the fact that the reality and function of the episcopal ministry have been preserved in many of these churches, with or without the title 'bishop'. Ordination, for example, is always done in them, by persons in whom the Church recognizes the authority to transmit the ministerial commission.

38. These considerations do not diminish the importance of the episcopal ministry. On the contrary, they enable churches which have not retained the episcopate to appreciate the episcopal succession as a sign, though not a guarantee, of the continuity and unity of the Church. Today churches, including those engaged in union negotiations, are expressing willingness to accept episcopal succession as a sign of the apostolicity of the life of the whole Church. Yet, at the same time, they cannot accept any suggestion that the ministry exercised in their own tradition should be invalid until the moment that it enters into an existing line of episcopal succession. Their acceptance of the episcopal succession will best further the unity of the whole Church if it is part of a wider process by which the episcopal churches themselves also regain their lost unity.

V. Ordination

A. The Meaning of Ordination

39. The Church ordains certain of its members for the ministry in the name of Christ by the invocation of the Spirit and the laying on of hands (I Tim. 4:14; II Tim. 1:6); in so doing it seeks to continue the mission of the apostles and to remain faithful to their teaching. The act of ordination by those who are appointed for this ministry attests the bond of the Church with Jesus Christ and the apostolic witness, recalling that it is the risen Lord who is the true ordainer and bestows the gift. In ordaining, the Church, under the inspiration of the Holy Spirit, provides for the faithful proclamation of the Gospel and humble service in the name of Christ. The laying on of hands is the sign of the

gift of the Spirit, rendering visible the fact that the ministry was instituted in the revelation accomplished in Christ, and reminding the Church to look to him as the source of its commission. This ordination, however, can have different intentions according to the specific tasks of bishops, presbyters and deacons as indicated in the liturgies of ordination.

40. Properly speaking, then, ordination denotes an action by God and the community by which the ordained are strengthened by the Spirit for their task and are upheld by the acknowledgment and prayers of the congregation.

B. The Act of Ordination

41. A long and early Christian tradition places ordination in the context of worship and especially of the eucharist. Such a place for the service of ordination preserves the understanding of ordination as an act of the whole community, and not of a certain order within it or of the individual ordained. The act of ordination by the laying on of hands of those appointed to do so is at one and the same time invocation of the Holy Spirit (*epiklesis*); sacramental sign; acknowledgment of gifts and commitment.

42. (a) Ordination is an invocation to God that the new minister be given the power of the Holy Spirit in the new relation which is established between this minister and the local Christian community and, by intention, the Church universal. The otherness of God's initiative, of which the ordained ministry is a sign, is here acknowledged in the act of ordination itself. 'The Spirit blows where it wills' (John 3:3): the invocation of the Spirit implies the absolute dependence on God for the outcome of the Church's prayer. This means that the Spirit may set new forces in motion and open new possibilities 'far more abundantly than all that we ask or think' (Eph. 3:20).

43. (b) Ordination is a sign of the granting of this prayer by the Lord who gives the gift of the ordained ministry. Although the outcome of the Church's *epiklesis* depends on the freedom of God, the Church ordains in confidence that God, being faithful to his promise in Christ, enters sacramentally into contingent, historical forms of human relationship and uses them for his purpose. Ordination is a sign performed in faith that the spiritual relationship signified is present in, with and through the words spoken, the gestures made and the forms employed.

44. (c) Ordination is an acknowledgment by the Church of the gifts of the Spirit in the one ordained, and a commitment by both the Church and the ordinand to the new relationship. By receiving the new minister in the act of ordination, the congregation acknowledges

the minister's gifts and commits itself to be open towards these gifts. Likewise those ordained offer their gifts to the Church and commit themselves to the burden and opportunity of new authority and responsibility. At the same time, they enter into a collegial relationship with other ordained ministers.

C. The Conditions for Ordination

45. People are called in differing ways to the ordained ministry. There is a personal awareness of a call from the Lord to dedicate oneself to the ordained ministry. This call may be discerned through personal prayer and reflection, as well as through suggestion, example, encouragement, guidance coming from family, friends, the congregation, teachers, and other church authorities. This call must be authenticated by the Church's recognition of the gifts and graces of the particular person, both natural and spiritually given, needed for the ministry to be performed. God can use people both celibate and married for the ordained ministry.

46. Ordained persons may be professional ministers in the sense that they receive their salaries from the church. The church may also ordain people who remain in other occupations or employment.

47. Candidates for the ordained ministry need appropriate preparation through study of scripture and theology, prayer and spirituality, and through acquaintance with the social and human realities of the contemporary world. In some situations, this preparation may take a form other than that of prolonged academic study. The period of training will be one in which the candidate's call is tested, fostered and confirmed, or its understanding modified.

48. Initial commitment to ordained ministry ought normally to be made without reserve or time limit. Yet leave of absence from service is not incompatible with ordination. Resumption of ordained ministry requires the assent of the Church, but no re-ordination. In recognition of the God-given charism of ministry, ordination to any one of the particular ordained ministries is never repeated.

49. The discipline with regard to the conditions for ordination in one church need not be seen as universally applicable and used as grounds for not recognizing ministry in others.

50. Churches which refuse to consider candidates for the ordained ministry on the ground of handicap or because they belong, for example, to one particular race or sociological group should re-evaluate their practices. This re-evaluation is particularly important today in view of the multitude of experiments in new forms of ministry with which the churches are approaching the modern world.

VI. Towards the Mutual Recognition of the Ordained Ministries

51. In order to advance towards the mutual recognition of ministries, deliberate efforts are required. All churches need to examine the forms of ordained ministry and the degree to which the churches are faithful to its original intentions. Churches must be prepared to renew their understanding and their practice of the ordained ministry.

52. Among the issues that need to be worked on as churches move towards mutual recognition of ministries, that of apostolic succession is of particular importance. Churches in ecumenical conversations can recognize their respective ordained ministries if they are mutually assured of their intention to transmit the ministry of Word and sacrament in continuity with apostolic times. The act of transmission should be performed in accordance with the apostolic tradition, which includes the invocation of the Spirit and the laying on of hands.

53. In order to achieve mutual recognition, different steps are required of different churches. For example:

a) Churches which have preserved the episcopal succession are asked to recognize both the apostolic content of the ordained ministry which exists in churches which have not maintained such succession and also the existence in these churches of a ministry of *episkopé* in various forms.

b) Churches without the episcopal succession, and living in faithful continuity with the apostolic faith and mission, have a ministry of Word and sacrament, as is evident from the belief, practice, and life of those churches. These churches are asked to realize that the continuity with the Church of the apostles finds profound expression in the successive laying on of hands by bishops and that, though they may not lack the continuity of the apostolic tradition, this sign will strengthen and deepen that continuity. They may need to recover the sign of the episcopal succession.

54. Some churches ordain both men and women, others ordain only men. Differences on this issue raise obstacles to the mutual recognition of ministries. But those obstacles must not be regarded as substantive hindrance for further efforts towards mutual recognition. Openness to each other holds the possibility that the Spirit may well speak to one church through the insights of another. Ecumenical consideration, therefore, should encourage, not restrain, the facing of this question.

55. The mutual recognition of churches and their ministries implies decision by the appropriate authorities and a liturgical act from which point unity would be publicly manifest. Several forms of such public act have been proposed: mutual laying on of hands, eucharistic con-

celebration, solemn worship without a particular rite of recognition, the reading of a text of union during the course of a celebration. No one liturgical form would be absolutely required, but in any case it would be necessary to proclaim the accomplishment of mutual recognition publicly. The common celebration of the eucharist would certainly be the place for such an act.

Commentary (9)

In the New Testament the term 'apostle' is variously employed. It is used for the Twelve but also for a wider circle of disciples. It is applied to Paul and to others as they are sent out by the risen Christ to proclaim the Gospel. The roles of the apostles cover both foundation and mission.

Commentary (11)

The basic reality of an ordained ministry was present from the beginning (cf. para. 8). The actual forms of ordination and of the ordained ministry, however, have evolved in complex historical developments (cf. para, 19). The churches, therefore, need to avoid attributing their particular forms of the ordained ministry directly to the will and institution of Jesus Christ.

Commentary (13)

These tasks are not exercised by the ordained ministry in an exclusive way. Since the ordained ministry and the community are inextricably related, all members participate in fulfilling these functions. In fact, every charism serves to assemble and build up the body of Christ. Any member of the body may share in proclaiming and teaching the Word of God, may contribute to the sacramental life of that body. The ordained ministry fulfils these functions in a representative way, providing the focus for the unity of the life and witness of the community.

Commentary (14)

The New Testament says very little about the ordering of the eucharist. There is no explicit evidence about who presided at the eucharist. Very soon however it is clear that an ordained ministry presides over the celebration. If the ordained ministry is to provide a focus for the unity of the life and witness of the Church, it is appropriate that an ordained minister should be given this task. It is intimately related to the task of guiding the community, i.e. supervising its life (episkopé) and strengthening its vigilance in relation to the truth of the apostolic message and the coming of the Kingdom.

Commentary (16)

Here two dangers must be avoided. Authority cannot be exercised without regard for the community. The apostles paid heed to the experience and the judgment of the faithful. On the other hand, the authority of ordained ministers must be so reduced as to make them dependent on the common opinion of the community. Their authority lies in their responsibility to express the will of God in the community.

Commentary (17)

The New Testament never used the term 'priesthood' or 'priest' (hiereus) to designate the ordained ministry or the ordained minister. In the New Testament, the term is reserved, on the one hand, for the unique priesthood of Jesus Christ and, on the other hand, for the royal and prophetic priesthood of all baptized. The priesthood of Christ and the priesthood of the baptized have in their respective ways the function of sacrifice and intercession. As Christ has offered himself, Christians offer their whole being 'as a living sacrifice'. As Christ intercedes before the Father, Christians intercede for the Church and the salvation of the world. Nevertheless, the differences between these two kinds of priesthood cannot be overlooked. While Christ offered himself as a unique sacrifice once and for all for the salvation of the world, believers need to receive continually as a gift of God that which Christ has done for them.

In the early Church the term 'priesthood' and 'priest' came to be used to designate the ordained ministry and minister as presiding at the eucharist. They underline the fact that the ordained ministry is related to the priestly reality of Jesus Christ and the whole community. When the terms are used in connection with the ordained ministry, their meaning differs in appropriate ways from the sacrificial priesthood of the Old Testament, from the unique redemptive priesthood of Christ and from the corporate priesthood of the people of God. St Paul could call his ministry 'a priestly service of the gospel of God, so that the offering of the Gentiles may be acceptable by the Holy Spirit' (Rom. 15:16).

Commentary (18)

Those churches which practise the ordination of women do so because of their understanding of the Gospel and of the ministry. It rests for them on the deeply held theological conviction that the ordained ministry of the Church lacks fullness when it is limited to one sex. This theological conviction has been reinforced by their experience during the years in which they have included women in their ordained ministries. They have found that women's gifts are as wide and varied as men's and that their ministry is a fully blessed by the Holy Spirit as the ministry of men. None has found reason to reconsider its decision.

Those churches which do not practise the ordination of women consider that the force of nineteen centuries of tradition against the ordination of women must not be set aside. They believe that such a tradition cannot be dismissed as a lack of respect for the participation of women in the Church. They believe that there are theological issues concerning the nature of humanity and concerning Christology which lie at the heart of their convictions and understanding of the role of women in the Church.

The discussion of these practical and theological questions within the various churches and Christian traditions should be complemented by joint study and reflection within the ecumenical fellowship of all churches.

Commentary (21)

The earliest Church knew both the travelling ministry of such missionaries as Paul and the local ministry of leadership in places where the Gospel was received. At local level, organizational patterns appear to have varied according to circumstances. The Acts of the Apostles mention for Jerusalem the Twelve and the Seven, and later James and the elders; and for Antioch, prophets and teachers (Acts 6:1–6; 15:13–22; 13:1). The letters to Corinth speak of apostles, prophets and teachers (I Cor. 12:28); so too does the letter to the Romans, which also speaks of deacons or assistants (Rom. 16:1). In Philippi, the secular terms episkopoi *and* diakonoi *were together used for Christian ministers (Phil. 1:1). Several of these ministries are ascribed to both women and men. While some were appointed by the laying on of hands, there is no indication of this procedure in other cases.*

Whatever their names, the purpose of these ministries was to proclaim the Word of God, to transmit and safeguard the original content of the Gospel, to feed and strengthen the faith, discipline and service of the Christian communities, and to protect and foster unity within and among them. These have been the constant duties of ministry throughout the developments and crises of Christian history.

Commentary (26)

These three aspects need to be kept together. In various churches, one or another has been over-emphasized at the expense of the others. In some churches, the personal dimension of the ordained ministry tends to diminish the collegial and communal dimensions. In other churches, the collegial or communal dimensions take so much importance that the ordained ministry loses its personal dimension. Each church needs to ask itself in what way its exercise of the ordained ministry has suffered in the course of history.

An appreciation of these three dimensions lies behind a recommendation made by the first World Conference on Faith and order at Lausanne in 1927: 'In view of (i) the place with the episcopate, the council of presbyters and the congregation of the faithful, respectively, had in the constitution of the early Church, and (ii) the fact that episcopal, presbyteral and congregational systems of government are each today, and have been for centuries, accepted by great communions in Christendom, and (iii) the fact that episcopal, presbyteral and congregations systems are each believed by many to be essential to the good order of the Church, we therefore recognize that these several elements must all, under conditions which require further study, have an appropriate place in the order of life of a reunited Church . . .'

Commentary (31)

In many churches there is today considerable uncertainty about the need, the rationale, the status and the functions of deacons. In what sense can the diaconate be considered part of the ordained ministry? What is it that distinguishes it from other ministries in the Church (catechists, musicians, etc.)? Why should deacons be ordained while these other ministries do not receive ordination? If they are ordained, do they receive ordination in the full sense of the word or is their ordination only the first step towards ordination as presbyters? Today, there is a strong tendency in many churches to restore the diaconate as an ordained ministry with its own dignity and meant to be exercised for life. As the churches move closer together there may be united in this office ministries now existing in a variety of forms and under a variety of names. Differences in ordering the diaconal ministry should not be regarded as a hindrance for the mutual recognition of the ordained ministries.

Commentary (34)

The apostles, as witnesses of the life and resurrection of Christ and sent by him, are the original transmitters of the Gospel, of the tradition of the saving words and acts of Jesus Christ which constitute the life of the Church. This apostolic tradition continues through history and links the Church to its origins in Christ and in the college of the apostles. Within this apostolic tradition is an apostolic succession of the ministry which serves the continuity of the Church in its life in Christ and its faithfulness to the words and acts of Jesus transmitted by the apostles. The ministers appointed by the apostles, and then the episkopoi of the churches, were the first guardians of this transmission of the apostolic tradition; they testified to the apostolic succession of the ministry which was continued through the bishops of the early Church in collegial communion with the presbyters and deacons within the Christian community. A distinction should be made, therefore, between the apostolic tradition of the whole Church and the succession of the apostolic ministry.

Commentary (36)

In the early Church the bond between the episcopate and the apostolic community was understood in two ways. Clement of Rome linked the mission of the bishop with the sending of Christ by the Father and the sending of the apostles by Christ (Cor. 42:44). This made the bishop a successor of the apostles, ensuring the permanence of the apostolic mission in the Church. Clement is primarily interested in the means whereby the historical continuity of Christ's presence is ensured in the Church thanks to the apostolic succession. For Ignatius of Antioch (Magn. 6:1, 3:1–2; Trall. 3:1), it is Christ surrounded by the Twelve who is permanently in the Church in the person of the bishop surrounded by the presbyters. Ignatius regards the Christian community assembled around the bishop in the midst of presbyters and deacons as the actual manifestation in the Spirit of the apostolic community. The sign of apostolic succession thus not only points to historical continuity; it also manifests an actual spiritual reality.

Commentary (39)

It is clear that churches have different practices of ordination, and that it would be wrong to single out one of those as exclusively valid. On the other hand, if churches are willing to recognize each other in the sign of apostolic succession, as described above, it would follow that the old tradition, according to which it is the bishop who ordains, with the participation of the community, will be recognized and respected as well.

Commentary (40)

The original New Testament terms for ordination tend to be simple and descriptive. The fact of appointment is recorded. The laying on of hands is described. Prayer is made for the Spirit. Different traditions have built different interpretations on the basis of these data.

It is evident that there is a certain difference between the unspoken cultural setting of the Greek cheirotonein and that of the Latin ordo or ordinare. The New Testament use of the former term borrows its basic secular meaning of 'appointment' (Acts 14:23; II Cor. 8:19), which is, in turn, derived from the original meaning of extending the hand, either to designate a person or to cast a vote. Some scholars see in cheirotonein a reference to the act of laying on of hands, in view of the literal description of the action in such seemingly parallel instances as Acts 6:6, 8:17, 13:3, 19:6, I Tim. 4:14; II Tim. 1:6. Ordo and ordinare, on the other hand, are terms derived from Roman law where they convey the notion of the special status of a group distinct from the plebs, as in the term ordo clarissimus for the Roman senate. The starting point of any conceptual construction using these terms will strongly influence what is taken for granted in both the thought and action which result.